VIVA ESPAÑA

Brian Stevenson

Country Books

Published by Country Books/Ashridge Press
Courtyard Cottage, Little Longstone, Bakewell, Derbyshire DE45 1NN
Tel: 01629 640670
e-mail: dickrichardson@country-books.co.uk
www.countrybooks.biz

ISBN 978-1-910489-06-2

© 2014 Brian Stevenson

The rights of Brian Stevenson as author of this work have
been asserted by him in accordance with the
Copyright, Designs and Patents Act 1993.

All rights reserved. No part of this publication may be reproduced,
stored in a retrieval system, or transmitted, in any way or form, or by
any means, electronic, mechanical, photocopying, or otherwise,
without the prior permission of the author and publisher.

British Library Cataloguing in Publication Data.
A catalogue record for this book is available from the British Library.

Printed and bound in England by 4edge Ltd. Hockley, Essex

Contents

Foreword	6
Just For A While	7
Airports	17
The Flight	21
Looking Around	26
Spanish Fever	34
The Lemon Express	46
Early Days	51
Eating Out	59
The Casa Pequena	66
Home and Away	71
Exploring Inland	78
The Skeleton and the She Devil	89

LEARNING SPANISH	96
ERNESTO – A DIVERSION	99
SOME FRIENDS	109
MOVING ON	113
FRESH FIELDS	117
ACKNOWLEDGEMENTS	120

The author, Brian Stevenson, and his wife, Eileen, in Poland 2004

Know ye the land of the cedar and vine,
Where the flowers ever blossom, and the beams ever shine;
Where the light winds of Zephyr, oppressed with perfume,
Wax faint o'er the gardens of Gul* in her bloom;
Where the citron and olive are fairest of fruit,
And the voice of the nightingale never is mute;
Where the tints of the earth, and the hues of the sky,
In colour, though varied, in beauty may vie;
And the purple of ocean is deepest in dye.

Byron

*The Rose.

Drawings by E. Stevenson.

Produced by Brian Stevenson
Meanwood Productions
Leeds, Yorkshire, Great Britain

First Edition, 1996.

FOREWORD

The names of a few of the people and places in the book have been changed for various reasons. For example, the name of 'Los Almendros,' or the almond trees is common along the Costa Blanca, but anyone who knows the district of Moraira will probably recognise the location at Tabaira.

In regard to the comments about Manchester airport. People unfamiliar with the French comedy films of the late Jacques Tati should know that he used to make fun of the de-humanising tendencies of certain aspects of modern times, as in the films 'Mon Oncle' and 'Traffic'.

About the property inspection visit at Calpe. It might not be completely accurate to say that there was no natural light in the apartment we saw. Memory can play tricks and we only spent a short time in the flat many years ago. However I do remember that it was very dark and have written the description in goodfaith.

In conclusion, since writing the book, the recent advent of the 'no frills' airlines such as Easyjet, or Jet2 at Leeds and Bradford airport, has made it easier to get cheaper and more convenient flights.

JUST FOR A WHILE

Eileen and I first visited Spain on a delayed honeymoon at the end of the nineteen fifties. We travelled with a firm called 'See Spain' overland by coach and train via London and Paris. We had to change stations in Paris but even then our 'See Spain' luggage labels seemed rather silly and open to ridicule. The 'See Spain' travel brochure invited you to 'look down on the wretches in the rain as you speed to your sunny destination by luxury coach'. In point of fact we had no desire whatever to look down on any 'wretches in the rain' although we did feel a bit like 'wretches in the rain ourselves' as we trudged around sightseeing at the resort of San Sebastian later in the holiday.

We arrived at our hotel after a rather tiring overnight journey. Our resort representative turned out to be a seemingly aristocratic middle-aged Spanish lady apparently down on her luck and forced to take any job she could get. Nevertheless she tried to be helpful and during the holiday arranged an evening out at a place she described as an 'exotic' night club called the 'Trinquete' (foremast). Unfortunately our expectations of the exotic were rather shattered when we discovered that most of our fellow revellers came from the British Rail goods depot at Wakefield not far from home.

The resort itself was interesting with lots to see and boasted a magnificent bay fringed by an extensive promenade shaded by plane trees. Unfortunately the weather was rather disappointing and similar to that in southern England, where were the vivid colours, the cloudless skies and the warm sunshine we had anticipated? However this was northern Spain and early in the season. Prices then were very cheap and some were still controlled, a cup of coffee costing as little as

six pesetas. Spanish cigarettes like the Bisante brand were very cheap indeed, but Virginia cigarettes were a luxury. We noticed that plastic products were still not available but luckily we had two spare plastic raincoats, which we gave to our representative. In spite of the mixed weather and the tedious journey we did enjoy the holiday in Spain and promised to return one day.

In spite of all our good intentions it would be another five years in the mid sixties before our next visit to Spain. We were booked on a package holiday to the Costa Brava along the Mediterranean coast. This area had been popularised by the film 'Pandora and the Flying Dutchman' around 1949. The package included overnight train travel from Calais; the age of the jet plane was just dawning. We finally arrived at the frontier town of Cerebra just as dawn was breaking. As soon as we disembarked, a whole crowd of our tourists ran pell-mell from the station down the hill for an included breakfast at a restaurant near the harbour. A women fell over in the rush and we stopped to help her, so by the time we reached the restaurant most of the food had gone. After this episode we relaxed by a placid peaceful sea as dawn broke. Then, after an hour or two we crossed the frontier into Spain and boarded the appropriate buses and taxis that were taking us to the different resorts. In contrast to our last visit we had arrived in the middle of a heat wave and this was the Spain we had dreamed about. Although it was still only September the crowds had gone home and the resort was quiet, so we made the most of the deserted swimming pools and the half empty beaches. The seawater was warm and clear making it suitable for snorkelling, an experience we hadn't experienced before. It turned out to be a holiday to remember for all the right reasons.

After this brilliant holiday we should have visited Spain again the following year, but again circumstances intervened. For the next few years we became interested in camping, which was quite fashionable just then. While still comparatively young we were able to put up with a certain amount of discomfort. Our first tent had a heavy metal frame and it was hard work erecting and dismantling it on one-night stands when touring. One year we packed everything into a Reliant three wheeler van, which we had at the time and set off for the continent. The van wasn't really very reliant because it would break down in heavy rain if water got into the electrical system by spray from the front wheel. Arriving at Calais as night fell we made for our first campsite at Berck Plage in Normandy. It wasn't really far but the French drivers flashing their headlights at us disturbed us. Unfortunately the excessive weight in the van had caused our headlights to point upwards, dazzling oncoming drivers. We only travelled by day after this. The Reliant van certainly caused some amusement as we made our way south towards the camping site at Valras Plage near Perpignan on the Mediterranean. This part of the coast is prone to high winds coming from the Pyrenees as we found out and a gale was howling as we drove into the camping site. We started to erect the tent, but couldn't get the tent pegs to hold in the soft sand and the tent kept blowing away. By this time we were getting tired and frustrated until a friendly camper told us about the special tent pegs that were needed around here. These were similar to cricket stumps, the only things that would hold down a tent. The gales continued and seemed to increase to hurricane force every night so after several days of buffeting we decided to strike camp. It was a great relief to reach the reach the peaceful and picturesque valley of the Dordogne where we found a good campsite and spent the rest of the holiday. What turned out to be our last camp took place in the mid-seventies at La Rochelle in western France. It was towards the end of August and the weather was perfect, with high temperatures inland, although the sea temperature of the Atlantic was cold. The camp was situated in the grounds of a chateau and its amenities included a shop, restaurant and a rather muddy lake suitable for swimming and fishing. Unusually, every evening at dusk a loud trumpet blast was played from the balcony at the front of the chateau. Although it was only the end of August we were surprised to find that the site was closing and everything was shutting down, so we were just in time.

 It would be about now that our next-door neighbour Ken and his wife sold their business in Leeds and retired to Spain at a place called Daimus on the Costa Blanca between Benidorm and Valencia. They had acquired two beachside apartments and were interested in selling one of them to us. Financial restrictions had just been lifted and so we booked a package holiday by plane to Benidorm to look around the area.

Since our first visit to San Sebastian years before, fundamental changes had taken place in many aspects of life both at home and abroad. Britain itself had become more prosperous and cheap charter flights and package holidays were becoming more and more popular. Spain itself was in the the thoes of economic change and after the death of Franco in 1975 corresponding political changes were taking place. Faced with immense problems, a modern democracy had come to power with the help of the new king and more tolerant politicians. Communications were improving steadily. For example, Alicante airport had only been developed in the sixties. A guidebook published about then mentioned a grass landing strip and recommended flying in by light plane from Madrid! At first Valencia airport was the only one for Benidorm. A Thomas Cook representative once told us about the difficulties of coach transfer from Valencia. This was especially true along the narrow roads and tunnels around Calpe before the autoroutes were built.

It would be fair to say that we were dazzled by the conditions at Benidorm. Everything seemed so bright and modern. Warm seas lapped the shores of Benidorm's two crescent shaped beaches of fine sand. Even commonplace things were of interest and to those who haven't seen it before, just the sight of oranges and lemons growing on trees is surprising. By this time Spain had a well-organised tourist industry able to cope with an increasing number of visitors. Building developments of all kinds were in progress up and down the coast and property for sale was readily available. The Estate Agents' shops in Benidorm displayed colourful photographs of different properties both new and second hand for sale at different prices. Some of these prices seemed very attractive and at the time you could get a studio apartment for as little as two thousand pounds.

Unfortunately, our neighbours apartment at Daimus was unsuitable, being just too far away from a convenient airport. However, this visit had increased our interest. On returning home we began sending for information and brochures about property on offer in different parts of Spain. Both the areas of the Costa del Sol and the Costa Blanca were particularly attractive. We noticed that some years before the World Health Organisation had described the Costa Blanca as being almost environmentally perfect with one of the healthiest climates in the world. It was this description that influenced our choice. Of course, the brightly coloured brochures and booklets we received painted a rosy picture of life on the Costa's. One production produced in Spain invited you to 'combine golf with underwater fishing'. With imagination running riot you picture a diver standing on the seabed with a golf club in hand about to take a shot. Hazards could include a wrecked galleon, a dangerous Moray eel in a bunker and a large lobster down the hole waiting to nip your fingers. Several of the brochures were targeted at senior citizens and carried pictures of smiling couples that had retired to this or to that Shangri-la. A typical article would read as follows:- 'Mr and Mrs Smith of Birmingham recently retired to Calpe on the Costa Blanca where they bought a villa last April. Every day the happy couple stroll gently down to the Voramar complex where they enjoy a quiet drink by the pool. Mr Smith is interested in gardening and is already surprised by the size of the tomatoes and the colourful flowers growing in his garden'.

No one can foretell the future and things were so different thirty or forty years ago. At that time other articles stressed the economic advantages of real estate. Capital values were said to be increasing by 'leaps and bounds' and the properties on offer selling like 'hot cakes', although I've never worked how fast hot cakes do sell for. Optimistic calculations were given showing how a generous income could be made from renting the property if desired. Indeed some of the firms that advertised appeared to be philanthropic organisations that only existed to give money away. It all reminded me of an old Laurel and Hardy film in which the two blockheads were going out to pay the rent of a house. On the way to do this they happened to pass an auction room where a sale is in progress. 'Come right in friends' calls a barker at the door sounding like a modern time-share tout. 'You can't go wrong, today we are giving things away!' 'Lets go in' says naïve Stan Laurel. 'We can't go wrong, today they are giving things away'. Of course the gullible pair are soon tricked into buying an old piano. A good-looking young woman approaches and asks them to bid on her behalf. She immediately disappears and before they know it they have made a bid and been lumbered with the white elephant. Finally, as the gormless couple attempt to carry away the old piano. A speeding lorry immediately runs over it and smashes it to smithereens on the road outside. When reading through these brochures and travel articles you inevitably come across the phrase 'breathtaking views'. It always amuses us when we come across this old cliche when used in this kind of writing.

In good times some firms used to run subsidised inspection trips to view overseas property. A specimen itinerary was provided for a typical visit which contained subtle marketing material. The prospective trip was described in glowing terms with photographs of happy clients arriving at a smart resort hotel. Sometimes personal recommendations were included. The second day was devoted to viewing property and finished with a sumptuous dinner at a first class restaurant. The final day got down to serious business with another viewing of favoured property if necessary. You were then invited to sign documents and pay a deposit. Of course, these trips only catered for the seriously interested and you were advised to have your finances organised before hand.

In recent years there have been very many television programmes about buying property or about living abroad. These programmes have titles like 'A Place in the Sun' or 'Wanted Down Under' and there was even a soap opera featuring Benidorm. There is a much wider choice of possible locations available today, but Spain remains the favourite place for people buying homes abroad, despite recent problems. These television programmes are broadcast at peak viewing times and are introduced by an attractive presenter with a name like Charlotte or Jasmine.

"I'm Charlotte Harvey and I'm helping Eddy and Joyce from Macclesfield choose a property here at Torrevieja on the Costa Brava in southern Spain. I've got four properties lined up for them to view a new apartment with a community pool, a rustic finca (farmhouse) in the campo, a town house inland and a detached villa near the coast. Are you planning to live out here permanently Joyce and what is your price range?"

"We could live out here permanently, but at the moment we're just thinking of holiday use and would like to rent out for some of the time. We have about sixty thousand pounds available, but could go higher if we see something we really like."

"Thank you, Joyce, and now I will hand you over to Ramon who will show you around this new apartment at the Playasol complex here in Torrevieja."

Ramon the estate agent takes over and shows Eddy and Joyce through the attractive panelled pine wood front door of the 'piso piloto' or show flat.

"This is the living room, notice the modern design and the windows that let in plenty of light."

"This is nice," comments Joyce and in fact the word 'nice' is repeated frequently as the tour proceeds and becomes a cliche like 'breathtaking views' in this kind of programme.

"This is the bathroom with shower and luxury fittings."

"Ooh, wow! Yes very nice indeed."

"This is the patio with breathtaking views towards the sea." "Oh, wow! It's really lovely, very very nice." The couple enthuse about everything they are shown and it looks as if they have found what they are looking for. However, Charlotte wants to give them a chance to see other properties, so next she takes them inland to see the rustic finca. The key word here is 'potential' which is also commonly used.

"This property is a bit run-down but comes with an orchard of orange and lemon trees and has great potential (again). There is an extension, which was used by the farmer's mule until very recently. I wouldn't go inside because there is still much evidence of his presence. The mule of course. However, the stable extension has the potential to be converted to an extra guest room or you could continue to use it for the mule. I am sure that the farmer would be willing to do a deal. If you are seriously interested I should have a surveyor take a look at the structure because there is a large crack in the outer wall. On the other hand, an Englishman recently bought a property like this, completely refurbished it, then sold it and made a profit."

"It certainly has potential," the couple reply, "but it would be far too much work for us and we definitely don't want a mule." The finca is obviously unsuitable, so Charlotte next takes them to see the town house in a nearby village.

"Prices are much cheaper inland and I thought you would be interested to see how much more you could get for your money out here." At first sight the house seemed quite spacious and attractive. The entrance consisted of wooden double doors big enough to admit a horse and donkey, which was their original purpose. Inside though, the rooms were very dark and some steep steps led up to the roof where there were panoramic views of the town and the countryside. Unfortunately, the house was situated right next to the village church and the loud clanging of bells suddenly interrupted the visit. All this certainly didn't thrill Eddy and Joyce, so they all went on to view the last property on the list, a luxury villa near the coast.

"This is a bit above your budget" says Charlotte, "but I thought you might be interested because of its position and letting possibilities. A villa like this one near the coast is easy to rent during the summer and it could help you to pay for any mortgage you might require." Eddy and Joyce are very impressed by the facilities on offer here and there follows another succession of 'very nice'and 'wow'.

"Yes, it's all really lovely," concludes Joyce, "even better than the first one we saw. It's a bit above our price range so we will have to think about this one very carefully."

At this stage the prospective buyers are often taken to meet some permanent residents at a social function, a barbecue or a meal at a restaurant. Funnily enough, these people always enthuse about the foreign lifestyle and the local climate and always say that they wouldn't dream of returning to Britain. One could almost suspect that they had been specially selected for this very occasion!

"Well" says Charlotte at the end of the programme, "have any of the properties we've seen attracted you."

"We didn't like the ruined finca with the stable for the mule, the town house was too dark and the clanging of the church bells would drive us mad. However, the luxury villa you showed us was very tempting and we're going to try and organise our finances and make an offer," they tell Charlotte.

"How exciting!" she replies and proceeds to ring the agent.

Unfortunately the offer is usually very low and the offer is invariable rejected. This is the moment of truth. Quite often the clients say that they really like the area, but need more time to look around. Some people are very enthusiastic about everything they are shown, but cool off disappointingly at the end. Others make a cheeky offer, which is usually rejected, with the vendor wanting more money for a property already greatly reduced in price. Sometimes the clients are just too slow to snap up an obvious bargain, not being properly prepared.

"We have to sell our own house first." So they get 'pipped at the post' by outsiders. None of these programmes were being shown in the late seventies, so then we just booked a package holiday to Benidorm to look around the area.

Agres – a mountain village

AIRPORTS

When we first started to visit Spain by air we had to travel all over the country to get a convenient flight, sometimes as far as Heathrow and Gatwick. Even the journey to Manchester airport wasn't easy along the busy, congested M62 motorway, and things don't seem to have changed that much today.

Manchester airport with its multiple terminals, endless escalators and huge, extensive buildings seems rather clinical and inhuman. The facilities are widely spaced out and if there is any chance of going to the wrong terminal you will do so. In fact, the place would make a good setting for a Jacques Tati French comedy film, which pokes fun at modern industry and conventions. Endless escalators and conveyors stretch in all directions and recorded voices record monotonously. 'This airport is a non-smoking zone, smoking is only allowed in designated areas which are clearly marked.'

You half expect to hear a voice announce in flat Daleck-like tones. 'Owners of unattended luggage will be exterminated'. Just recently Manchester airport has acquired an example of the very latest in cutting edge technology. This important innovation comes in the form of a robotic floor cleaner or a 'moppet' as it has been named. The machine runs on batteries, which have a life of about twelve hours. We are told that the contraption is interactive and has a musical female voice, which addresses any passengers in its path with a polite request. 'Please would you move out of the way?'

If you refuse to move the 'moppet' doesn't make a fuss but just cleans around you. However, as we all know, machines eventually go wrong. So I hope I am not there on the day when the 'moppet' malfunctions and tries to mop and scrub anyone in its way whilst losing its temper and shouting at the travellers.

Perhaps the function of the machine could be developed by converting the 'moppet' into a kind of mobile Madam Tussauds, disguising it in different ways to commemorate important days or famous people. For example, to mark the French National Day on July 14th, the 'moppet' could be dressed up as Napoleon, as thy do with the famous fountain called the Manikin Pis in Brussels. One July, a large crowd had gathered in front of the Manikin to observe the ceremony. The band began to play the French National Anthem, the Marseillaise, and just as the music reached a crescendo, 'let vengeance nerve our hands', someone turned on the water stopcock full on by mistake. An immense jet of water suddenly shot out of Napoleon's trousers and drenched the crowd, which jumped back in alarm. Other roles for the 'moppet' could include famous sportsmen or women, celebrities and even politicians.

Today, we much prefer to use Leeds/Bradford airport when we travel. It's much nearer home and there isn't the same hustle and bustle and the crowds one finds at Manchester. Many airports are in the process of making improvements and extensions. In Yorkshire, Leeds/Bradford airport started out as just a big field at Yeadon, a suburb of north Leeds. I remember visiting Yeadon airport as it was called then as a child before the Second World War. We were there to observe the antics of the dangerously underpowered and ungainly machines like the 'Flying Flea' or peoples aircraft as it was called at the time. One such aircraft got into difficulties as it attempted to take off. The plane started its run at the far side of field, but seemed unable to increase its speed. We watched fascinated as the plane lumbered across the airfield. It gradually reached the boundary where it made a desperate convulsive leap over the hedge and subsided like a flat Yorkshire pudding in the next field. However, one reliable aircraft in those far off days was the twin-engined bi-plane, the De Havilland Dragon Rapide. Before the Second World War Dragon Rapides operated a regular passenger air service between Yeadon and the Isle of Man. One day our family flew on one of these flights. In those days the slightest thing could cause a delay and the flight was postponed on the

The author at Yeadon (Leeds/Bradford) airport in 1938

first day because it was raining. We returned on the second day and the sun came out as we waited in what passed for the terminal building, but which seemed like a large garage. The Dragon only carried seven or eight passengers, but everything was fine as we took off and headed towards Blackpool where we had to re-fuel. The plane seemed to fly very low, which gave superb views of the Skipton Gap and Pendle Hill. We landed safely at Blackpool airport in front of a surprisingly large and interested crowd and soon took off again to fly over the Irish Sea. Again, the plane flew low and we had some good views of the ferries coming out of Fleetwood. The whole flight was a memorable experience, but the Second World War broke out soon afterwards, putting an end to civil aviation at Yeadon for well over a decade.

The recent increase in the number of airports throughout the country reminds me of a once popular custom years ago. In the nineteen-fifties it was the fashion to collect brightly coloured plastic pennants to stick on car windows, windscreens or bumpers. The pennants carried messages and slogans advertising different holiday resorts or tourist attractions. 'We have seen the lions of Longleat, we have seen Chester Zoo, and we have been to Woolacombe Sands' etc. Perhaps something like this could be revived with the different airports issuing their own pennants with relevant slogans such as:- 'We have survived Manchester airport, we lost our luggage at Luton, we've seen Leeds and Bradford airport' etc. Even foreign airports could be included with appropriate slogans like:- 'We got stranded at Alicante' or 'we spent the night at Malaga'. Some of the rarer pennants from places like Southampton on Tyne-Tees could become collector's items and quite valuable in time.

At the time of this property inspection trip to Benidorm there were no flight available from our local airport, so we were forced to book a holiday from Manchester, which was often the case in those days. After a comfortable flight and an easy transfer we finally arrived at the Hotel Playamar in Benidorm, which was to be our inspection tour base.

La Mata Rascasa development, September 2002.
We were here for ten years

THE FLIGHT

The check-in queues at airports seem to have the same characteristics as those at supermarket tills. There are usually three or four alternative queues and you always seem to choose the wrong one. You shuffle forward painfully slowly, hoping there will be no problem to hold things up. Your heart sinks if there is some kind of technical hitch like a lost passport, with people ransacking their bags in an effort to find it. Meanwhile the next queue forges ahead quickly, leaving you standing. Then, most infuriatingly, as in a supermarket, another checkout opens nearby. There's a sudden surge of people behind you and as it say in the good book: 'Those who would be first shall be last and those who are last shall be first.' At last, with passports and tickets in hand you arrive at the check-in desk. At this stage you are asked to put your luggage on the conveyor belt and questioned about the contents of your cabin baggage that you are taking on the plane. Nowadays anything sharp and even the tiniest nail scissors are all confiscated. Looking around we are surprised at the size of cases some people take on holiday, all seem much bigger than ours. Also, if there is a size limit for cabin baggage it doesn't seem to be enforced. Some people carry large heavy bags or rucksacks, which they heave into the cabin racks just above your head. Not so long ago we saw a large case, which had split open on the carousel at Alicante airport revealing that the case was stuffed with tins of baked beans. Perhaps the passenger thought he was travelling to some third world country where there was a famine.

Your passports are checked three or four times and compared with flight tickets and boarding cards, then it's on to the x-ray machines. You have to get rid of any metal objects on your person such as keys coins or belts, even certain kinds of shoes can alert the machine. If the metal archway 'pings' as you go through, a serious looking official steps forward to make a search and you feel quite guilty for some reason. Your hand baggage has to pass through another security device and an innocent object such as a paint box alerts the machine, triggering off another security search as the suspicious bag is ransacked. When some bags are searched it's like opening Pandora's Box when all kinds of objects are disgorged. There could be anything from boxes of sweets, assorted groceries or what appears to be the entire stock of a Superdrug store. You could make up a poem about all this, with apologies to John Masefield:

> 'Battered British baggage with a worn out zipper
> Passing through the customs in the mad March days
> With a cargo of tea bags, biscuits, perfume
> Liquorice allsorts and Cadbury's Milk Trays'

It's a relief when you hear the flight number called: 'Will all passengers on the Jet 2 flight to Alicante please proceed to gate number four'. Boarding the plane takes some time, but at last everyone is settled. Before take off the cabin crew point out the plane exits and a safety video is shown. I am always intrigued when the stewardess explains how to 'top up the air in a life jacket by blowing through a rubber tube and attracting attention by blowing on a whistle'. It all reminds me of a cartoon in an old pre-war Punch magazine. On a cinema screen the hero in the film is pictured rescuing the heroine by making a daring mid-air jump from the wing of one old bi-plane to another. The young man says to his girl friend: 'Certainly I would Darling, but in our case I hope it won't be necessary'. In our case too, we really hope it won't ever be necessary to 'top up the air in a life jacket and attract attention by blowing on a whistle'.

The passengers you meet on these holiday flights are usually pleasant. We met one such couple on a flight from Manchester, they seemed to share all our interests, but were travelling to a different resort in another direction. For some reason we didn't get around to exchanging addresses, thinking we would see them again at the end of the week. Sadly, they didn't appear on the return flight, which ended a budding friendship. Fate was against us on this occasion. You heart sinks if the passenger in the next seat asks: 'How much did you pay for your flight?' We know exactly what's coming next because whatever amount you say, they will always come up with something better. 'Did you pay as much as that,' comes the inevitable reply, 'we paid a lot less and we only booked last week.' Sometimes the pressurisation of the planes cabin can cause problems. On one flight to Valencia a young women had bought a packet of potato crisps, which she placed in front of her. As the plane gained height the bag started to expand until it suddenly exploded with a loud pop. Fragments of crisps showered all over nearby passengers, much to everyone's annoyance! However, these events lay in the future and this flight was completely normal. The plane banked as we approached Alicante airport and a baked khaki coloured landscape unfolded beneath us dotted by tiny white houses with adjoining pools looking like miniature blue postage stamps. The plane descended still further and there was a rumble from the undercarriage, a glimpse of tarmac through the window, a jolt and a roar from the retro-jets. We had landed. Today, the journey from the airport to the resort takes just over an hour along the autopista. However, at that time we had to drive through Alicante itself because the autopista stopped north of the city. In compensation the old route was quite interesting as it skirted the splendid palm shaded mosaic promenade stretching alongside the harbour with its yachts and commercial shipping. At the place where the Playa del Postiguet begins there is a roundabout and the Hotel Palas where we endured perhaps the most uncomfortable night of our lives. We occupied accommodation facing the roundabout and it was impossible to sleep as the traffic braked and accelerated just below the windows of our room. At times it seemed as if the lorries were coming right inside the room itself! A little way past here is the lift to the castle of Santa Barbara, which dominates the city. This site has been fortified since pre-historic times and is said to be almost untakable. The British garrisoned it during the war of the Spanish Succession in 1707. The besieging French army prepared an mine, said to be big enough to destroy the entire rock and invited the British garrison to surrender. The British refused, so there was an immense explosion and when the dust settled half the cliff had disappeared, but the gallant British troops still held out. Further along here the N322 road passes the terminus of the Trenet narrow gauge railway of which more later, before striking inland towards the southern end of the autopista. Having reached the motorway our coach made good progress as it bi-passed the coastal suburbs of Alicante such as Campello and San Juan before skirting the town of Villajoyosa noted for its chocolate products and its rugby club amongst other things. After Villajoyosa the sight of the split rock at the summit of the Sierra Nevada heralds the skyline of Benidorm. There are one or two tales about the origin of this rock. One story has it that the mythical giant Roland cut the rock with his sword and tossed it into the sea in a temper. There it lies today as Peacock Island, a modern tourist attraction.

When Rose Macauley, the author of the classic book 'Fabled Shores' drove down this way after the Second World War she remarked on the

A 'finca' in the hills

absence of British people and said that she'd seen only one GB car and that was near the frontier. She described the land around Benidorm as poor and barren and the coast itself as an open door for smugglers. One wonders what she would think if she could see the resort today, the changes over the last fifty years have been unimaginable. Today, Benidorm is said to boast the tallest building in Spain, the gigantic Hotel Bali 2 that stands out as you approach the town. We saw the building in the process of construction several years ago, although even then there didn't seem much urgency about the project, as small gang of men were fitting windows, assisted by a crane of immense height. At that time the construction was said to have been in progress for five years. We had to wait before arriving at our hotel the Playamar because the bus had to make a circuit of several other hotels first. There was the unfortunately named Hotel Titanic and then a succession of other hotels, each name beginning with the letter R, the Rio Park, the Reymar and the Riudor. We were last on the list before we arrived finally at our hotel which was to our base for the next two weeks.

At Casa Cervera between La Mata and Torrevieja

LOOKING AROUND

The Playamar was situated on rising ground behind the Poniente beach, the southernmost of Benidorm's two sweeping crescent shaped beaches. The hotel boasted a large outdoor swimming pool, a spacious lounge for evening entertainment and a generously sized bowling green for older clients. During the winter months important bowling competitions were organised at the Playamar. Messages from well-known tourist firms were displayed on notice boards in the foyer and different tour representatives visited the hotel each day for what were called 'Welcome Parties'. These occasions were used to sell tickets for various excursions and to advertise 'Blanket Tours' which were free of charge. Free tea was on offer every afternoon at four o'clock and some holidaymakers used to return to the hotel from far and wide every day just to get this free tea.

The day after our arrival at the Playamar, Eileen and I began our property search. Not wishing to waste time we called in at a local estate agency named 'Alexanders' and they were very helpful. They showed us a variety of properties around Benidorm including some studio apartments at a development called 'New Life 3,' 'New Life 1 and 2' were next door. The apartment we saw had been well prepared for sale with new furniture, modern light fittings and smart light coloured walls. Although on the small side, the apartment made a good impression and it would have bee a sensible purchase at only about two thousand pounds at that time. Unfortunately, this good impression was rather spoilt by a water leak visible in the bathroom ceiling from the flat above.

The next day we had made arrangements to meet a representative of

The road to Benidorm a hundred years ago?

a large local building firm, based at the town of Benisa to the north of Benidorm, at our hotel. Eileen and I waited patiently in the hotel foyer as the minutes ticked by but no one arrived. After about an hour we got tired of waiting and if we had left just then the course of our lives would have taken a completely different direction.

"They're not coming," I said to Eileen, "we've waited long enough, let's go and look at some other property."

We stood up to leave when a youngish looking Spanish man hurried through the hotel entrance. He was smartly dressed, quite tall with regular features and dark hair. He seemed about thirty years old and wore two golden signet rings on his left hand. We found out later that he spoke fluent English and had an English wife. The man went up to the reception desk. "I have an appointment to meet two English people here this morning and I wonder if there have been any messages." "We think that must be us we exclaimed." "I am sorry I am late, but I was delayed in Moraira," explained the man. We shook hands and introduced ourselves. "I am Antonio from 'Construcciones Benisa' and I have come to take you in, I take in all the British clients." This startled us a little. "We expected to be taken in by the people in Spain, but we didn't expect you to be so open about it all." "No, no!" protested Antonio, "you don't understand, I've come to take you into the office and to show you around the district. My colleague takes all the Germans in too."

"We're pleased to hear that the Germans get taken in too" we replied, "they probably deserve it."

"I think we will visit Altea first" said Antonio, ignoring this remark, "we have some property there and it's on the way to Calpe and Moraira."

We got up and followed Antonio to a large Mercedes car standing outside the hotel. We found out later that Antonio always had a large, powerful car; impressions and prestige are important things in Spain. We got into the car and Antonio drove us rapidly out of Benidorm towards the town of Altea about ten miles away. The charming blue dome of the local church sparkled in the sunshine and as we approached the town Antonio began telling us things that he imagined would be of interest. 'Altea has a nudist beach and many artists,' he announced as if the two things went together in a kind of symbiotic relationship. In actual fact Altea has an impressive history and was an important Phoenician port in ancient times. Today, it has a lively town centre, a picturesque old quarter at the top of the hill and a thriving Tuesday market in the port area visited by coach parties from Benidorm. On Sundays and fiestas a somewhat dangerous variation of the game of pelota is played in the narrow streets near Altea's church square. Players strike the ball hard with their bare hands against walls, doors and windows, which unlike the crowds of spectators are protected by stout grills!

Antonio turned left at the traffic lights in the town centre and drove up a hill at one side of the town. After various twists and turns we arrived at an area overlooking the sea with views towards Benidorm in the distance. Quite a lot of Continental people seem to favour this kind of location with an emphasis on height and long distance views and it doesn't seem to matter if the place is inconveniently situated and a long way from facilities like shops. We have seen many villas and houses along the Costa Blanca perched on the tops of mountains, overhanging sheer cliffs and other wildly inaccessible places where you would think it impossible to build anything at all, which had all been sold and occupied.

The properties we had come to see consisted of block of town houses with long distance views at the front and a view of the local cemetery at the side. This wasn't necessary a drawback because Spanish cemeteries usually consist of a pleasant tree-shaded courtyard enclosed by high stonewalls with niches along the sides for the deceased. The niches are often decorated with flowers and display a small photograph of the occupant. There are no ugly gravestones and in fact if one must think along these lines a Spanish cemetery would make a tranquil final resting place.

Apart from the views, these town houses at Altea didn't seem to have very much going for them. The design of the show house appeared to be very ordinary as we approached the front door up a steep flight of steps with a rickety banister rail. There was nothing much to impress us inside and Eileen, who knows about these things, declared that the colour scheme was all wrong.

"They are popular with the Germans, but expensive for what they are and not really worth the money," admitted Antonio with surprising candour. We agreed with him and crossed off the town houses, noting Antonio's sincere and honest approach, which continued for as long as we knew him.

Our next 'port of call' was at Calpe about another ten kilometres along the coast where there were some apartments to view at what Antonio called an 'interesting' price. Between Altea and Calpe the mountain ranges come right down to the seashore and the N322 road, the autopista and the narrow gauge railway all have to tunnel through the mountainside. One can still see a section of the old road here with narrow bridges and dark tunnels, showing what things must have been like in the past. Just before reaching Calpe we passed the imposing entrance to the multi-million pound Maryvilla estate built on the north-facing slope of a great headland jutting out into the sea towards Ibiza. Antonio told us that the sight of this prestige development had the Spanish Minister for Tourism wringing his hands in despair, because it had been built in entirely the wrong place. Nearly all these luxury villas with pools on Maryvilla are left in the shade after mid-day during the winter.

The resort of Calpe is said to have been founded by some Spanish refugees fleeing from Gibralter, who saw its resemblance to their former home and is dominated by the towering rock of the Penon d'Ifach, which rises to the height of over a thousand feet. Calpe was once just a small fishing village and in fact nearly all the popular resorts along the coast seem to have started out as 'just a fishing village,' including Benidorm, as every guide book tells you. This well-worn phrase of 'just a fishing village' has now become something of a cliche like 'breathtaking views'. Fishing is still important but has become overshadowed by tourism in recent times. About fifty years ago Calpe consisted of two distinct areas, the town centre up the hill near the main road and the fishing port nestling under of the shadow of the Penon d'Ifach about a mile away. Over the years building developments have caused the two areas to coalesce, joined up by new roads, apartment blocks, hotels and a smart beachside promenade. The town now extends well beyond the port, stretching behind the Levante beach in the direction of Fustera cove two miles further on.

We entered Calpe, turning off the N322 and drove down the bustling main street, stretching down the hill to the sea front. We drove about half way down the hill until Antonio pulled up in front of an apartment block with shops at street level. Getting got out of the car, Antonio produced a bunch of keys and unlocked an unobtrusive door at the side of a shop. We entered the door and mounted a flight of steps, which led up to a long corridor illuminated by a very dim bulb, something like the emergency lighting in a submarine. It all looked rather sinister and menacing and you could imagine a serial killer lurking there late at night as in American films shown after nine o'clock by Channel 5. Suddenly the light went out and we were plunged into pitch darkness.

We heard Antonio clicking switches and the dim light flickered on again. "There is a time switch of two minutes here to save electricity," he explained.

"It may save electricity, but it's ruining our nerves" we replied.

Producing another key from the large bunch Antonio unlocked a door at the end of the corridor, turned on a light and showed us into a spacious apartment, which was like entering another world. The apartment was very well appointed with a fitted kitchen, refrigerator, expensive looking orange coloured marble tiled floors and Roca sanitary ware in the bathroom. There were two bedrooms of a generous size and a dual-purpose living room cum dining area.

"These apartments are excellent value, close to all facilities and within your price range" said Antonio, "we have already sold some to English clients."

The apartments certainly seemed a bargain, but we wondered why they were going so cheaply. Warning bells began to ring in our heads and we remembered the old saying: 'If something seems too good to be true then it probably is' and suddenly the reason for this apparent bargain began to dawn on us.

"Aren't there any windows in here, and must you have the light on all the time?" we asked.

Antonio replied as plausibly as he could. "Well, you see the next apartment block is situated very close to this one, and as there is no view we didn't think it necessary to include any windows. But you won't notice it very much if you are down on the beach most of the time and as you can see it's very convenient here, near the shops and the town centre."

Antonio was an excellent salesman, but even he couldn't sell us this concept.

"No thank you," we replied, "we don't want to live in artificial light; it would be like being in a prison. Please can we go on to see the property near Moraira that you mentioned earlier?" So we returned back down Stephen King's nightmare corridor into the dazzling light

Going home from Market

on Calpe's main street. Just as we were driving off, an English voice shouted down the street; "Hey, I want to speak to you," but Antonio only waved and drove off hurriedly. "Who was that?" we asked curiously. "Just an English client," he replied diplomatically, "but I haven't time to see him right now."

We wondered why the man wanted to see Antonio so urgently; perhaps he had just found out that there were no windows in his apartment.

Moraira, Costa Blanca

SPANISH FEVER

Having escaped the attentions of the English client, we drove down Calpe's main street and turned right along the dual carriageway of the coastal road with some saltpans to the left and newly built areas to the right. After passing the turn-off to the port area and the Penon d'Ifach, the road narrowed and began to follow the indentations of the coastline, skirting tiny coves, obscure beaches and estates of flower-decked villas.

The road between Calpe and Moraira is officially a route of special tourist attraction, but it would need a writer with the descriptive talents of an author like Lady Fortescue to do justice to the scenery to around here. Long before Peter Mayle's famous book 'A Year in Provence' was published Lady Fortescue wrote the best selling book 'Perfume from Provence' set in the pre-war French Riviera that provided escapist reading for a British public reeling from the effects of the world depression and still traumatised by memories of the Great War of 1914 to 1918. The book gave an amusing and touching account about setting up house and about life in southern France in the nineteen thirties. Sir John Fortescue had been badly injured in a gas attack during the Great War and left seriously ill. It was these injuries, a gentler climate and a favourable exchange rate at the time that prompted the couple to live in southern France. Even today, health, money and climate are given as the main reasons for emigrating to Spain.

As we progressed beyond Calpe, Antonio swung the big Mercedes expertly around the tight corners and across the narrow bridges of the tortuous route. Ahead, a switchback line of blue-grey hills dipped down into the haze of the shimmering sea at the point of Moraira. The

Mediterranean sea blazed and scintillated as if some mythical god had poured in all the precious stones of the world. There were colourful tones of emerald and sapphire over deep water, turquoise and aquamarine over hidden sandbanks, amethyst near submerged rocks and sparkling diamonds where the sun touched the ripples. We were on our way to see the Tabaira urbanisation built by Construcciones Benisa about a mile outside the lovely village of Moraira.

"We can view the property first and then have some lunch at the clubhouse," Antonio suggested.

Urbanisations are estates of brand new property, typically built on the most unlikely terrain, very poor agricultural land, barren scrub, and virgin pinewoods or on rocky mountains inland. Many of these developments are comparatively isolated and some way from a village or other habitations, so facilities like a supermarket, a clubhouse/restaurant, a swimming pool and tennis courts have to be included in the plan as added attractions. Some of these developments seem very speculative and ambitious, yet most are surprisingly successful. Of course, much preliminary work has to be done first before building work can begin with the construction of roads and the provision of utilities like water and electricity, so a vast amount of capital is involved. Perhaps one of the biggest developments on the Costa Blanca is situated on the windy heights of the barren foothills that shelter Moraira. Here, at a place called 'El Cumbre del Sol' (pinnacle of the sun) is a scheme involving the creation of what is virtually a small town.

About forty years ago a local building firm with German connections acquired an extensive barren tract of hilly scrubland, gullies and cliffs with scarcely enough vegetation to feed a herd of goats, along the coastline between Moraira and the neighbouring village of Benitachell. At first new roads were put in to open up the area and a whole hillside blasted away to give access to a previously landlocked cove. From Benitachell a signpost points the way along a wide road, constructed with admirable skill and boldness that climbs bravely up the trackless hillside to the breezy heights of the plateau above. Up here there are superb long distance views inland and a glorious vista of the whole bay of Javea with the Mongo moutain behind. The main entrance to 'El Cumbre del Sol' with some administrative buildings and a sales office is situated a little further along the road. Just past here is a road junction with a signpost directing traffic to different parts of the estate. One road leads down to the clubhouse/restaurant, swimming pool and commercial centre. A second steep, twisting road descends down the hill and eventually arrives at a sheltered cove with a beach of mixed sand and pebbles. There is a seasonal cafe/bar here and a surprisingly spacious car park, but it must have been very lonely and secluded down here in olden times and a haven for smugglers.

From this beach you can look upwards and see grandiose villas, some as big as small castles, tottering on the very edge of the towering cliffs. Some of these millionaire villas have film star swimming pools built on stilt-like columns of concrete and actually overhanging the precipice. Certainly, it isn't a place for the faint hearted or for anyone suffering from vertigo. Any kind of a cliff fall or an earth tremor would cause a disaster. Yet the development is not exclusively up-market and the property available is surprisingly varied, ranging from hotel-like villas to economy terrace bungalows. Many of the larger villas have beautiful sub-tropical gardens with mature palm trees and it must have

Moraira – Costa Blanca

cost a small fortune to import the necessary earth to make this possible because the sub-strata here is just bare rock. The whole development stretches right along the coast to Moraira itself, yet in spite of all the building work, there must be enough land to last to last for at least another hundred years. Just like the apartments at Altea, the main attractions here are the views and the elevated location. However, it can be chilly up here in winter and rather lonely as well, because most of the accommodation is used only for holidays in the summer.

The 'Tabaira' urbanisation that Eileen and I were going to see was on a much smaller scale and entirely different in character to 'El Cumbre del Sol'. Before reaching Moraira, Antonio turned off the winding coastal road into a maze of by-roads that meandered through shady woods of Mediterranean pines. We passed a velvet turfed nine-hole golf course, a backwoods supermarket and various types of white-washed villas basking in the sun. After a short time we arrived at a clearing in the woods with nothing in sight except a small, pretty little villa, white as icing sugar, with a neat porch and surrounded by clumps of agaves, wild herbs and rosemary. It looked just like something out of a fairytale.

"It reminds me of Hansel and Gretel's cottage made of sweets and barley sugar," I whispered to Eileen. "Do you think I should ask Antonio if a wicked witch or a woodcutter named Grendel own villas nearby? Perhaps Little Red Riding Hood passes this way through the woods on the way to her grandmother's cottage. Also, I've heard that wolves still live in the forests of Spain."

"We've built this little villa as a speculation," said Antonio, interrupting this chain of thoughts, "and it's ready for immediate occupation. I'd like to show you the interior so you can appreciate the quality of the fixtures and fittings."

Antonio unlocked the handcrafted panelled pinewood front door and we entered the little house warily, half expecting the exposed wooden roof beams to be made of liquorice, the kitchen unit's gingerbread, the bath barley sugar and the wicked witch lurking in a cupboard ready to spring out.

In fact, the design of the little villa or 'casa pequena' as Antonio called it was very simple and functional. Lengthways, one half of the house served as a pleasant living area with an open plan kitchen and breakfast bar at one end. The other half of the house was divided into two bedrooms with the bathroom in between. There were floors of different coloured marble tiles and a stone fireplace halfway along the inside wall of the living room. The exposed wooden beams in the bedrooms and in living room, combined with the ornate wrought-iron wall and ceiling lights enhanced the Spanish effect. Iron grills and wooden shutters guarded the windows whilst the roof was finished with local red terracotta tiles. We began to feel quite excited; this was the most interesting property we had seen so far.

After inspecting the living area, the kitchen and the two bedrooms, Antonio led the way into the bathroom where we were greeted by an incredible sight. There, suspended above the bath and secured by a few thin wires hung a large hot-water cylinder. A veritable Sword of Damocles.

"I wouldn't bathe under that," said Eileen, "it looks as if the whole lot could come crashing down at any minute."

We had to think about all this very carefully because there were plenty of good points about the little house. It was certainly attractive, well-designed and immediately available, but in the end it was the cylinder in the bathroom that was to prove the deciding factor.

"We're sorry, Antonio, the villa is very nice, but it does seem rather isolated and cut off around here and we don't like the layout in the bathroom very much."

By this time it was almost two o'clock and Antonio invited us to go for a meal at the Tabaira clubhouse. We discovered later that he could offer two separate meals as inducements to prospective clients. Leaving Hansen and Gretel's gingerbread house, we returned to the estate road and after traversing a labyrinthine maze of tracks, drove up a steep hill flanked by impressive villas designed in the Andalucian style with arches, curved walls and spacious patios. Some of these villas had quaint names displayed in fancy wrought iron letters on gates, house walls or beside front doors. There was a 'Droomland' (presumably dreamland in Dutch), 'Los Muchachos' (the kids), one or two 'Vistamars' or terrible made up names like 'Lynbarry's', 'Johnspad', 'Bridiana' or 'Micasa'. Apart from the names, it was sometimes possible to tell the nationality of the owners from the outside appearance of a villa. For example, an American owned villa would have a steer's head above the front door, something like a ranch in 'Dallas'. An obviously German villa would display crenulated garden walls, a heavy iron gate, an ornate archway and a pretentious pair of concrete lions or gryphons perched on top of the gateposts.

There were often warning signs on the gates depicting a lurid picture of a fat pop-eyed bulldog suffering what appeared to be a fit of apoplexy whilst foaming at the mouth. Another sign illustrated a fleeing burglar carrying a sack of loot having his trousers seat torn off by a ferocious dog resembling the 'Hound of the Baskervilles'. The pictures were accompanied by captions in Spanish such as 'perro peligroso' (dangerous dog) or 'perro malo' (bad dog). When these 'dangerous' dogs appeared they often turned out to be tiny Yorkshire terriers, nervous toy poodles or miniature dachshunds and quite harmless.

The estate road levelled out at the top of the hill and arrived on a plateau overlooking a valley rich with vines and almond groves and with long distance views of Calpe rock and the adjacent mountains. Later on these mountains would become clothed with white newly built villas, but just then only pinewoods could be seen. The stone-clad Tabaira clubhouse stood on a slight incline on the crest of the hill with a large swimming pool in front and surrounded by lush landscaped subtropical gardens. An isolated looking supermarket had been built on a level site next to the road just below, the nucleus of a commercial centre. We noticed that the grass on the lawns surrounding the swimming pool appeared to be brown and dead and we asked Antonio how this had happened.

"Well," replied Antonio, "one of the partners in the firm Senor Pepe gave orders that the water in the swimming pool should be re-cycled when the pool was drained for servicing. We knew what was likely to happen, but no one wanted to argue with the boss. So the pool was emptied and the water used to irrigate the lawns. Unfortunately, the chlorine in the water immediately killed off all the grass, hence the bare desert. If anyone else had been responsible there would have been uproar."

Skirting the incredibly beautiful grounds full of exotic plants we drove around to the car park at the front of the clubhouse. We got out of the car and walked through the entrance doors, passing a long bar to the left. A hallway led out into a magnificent restaurant with exposed roof beams and discreet alcoves along the walls. Meticulously polished silver cutlery and expensive looking crystal goblets sparkled on the snow-white tablecloths, whilst vases filled with local wild flowers added a touch of colour. Antonio told us that all the restaurant staff had been trained at the expense of Construcciones Benisa.

"We wanted a high standard of service," he explained, "and there just wasn't the experienced staff available in the village." Another staircase led up to a second floor where there was a library and a games room for the convenience of guests. A large function room built on the other side of the clubhouse could accommodate dinner/dances and other social events.

Of course, these were the salad days at Tabaira and we were seeing everything at its best. Unfortunately, nothing lasts forever and when most of the urbanisation had been completed the company became more interested in new projects. A year or two later the clubhouse was leased out and a refreshment kiosk built next to the pool. A little later this area around the pool was fenced off and charges began to be made for the use of the swimming facilities. Finally, around 1986, everything closed down and the clubhouse and the grounds lay forlorn and neglected until several years later when the entire complex was sold off as a private residence. A similar situation occurred at another urbanisation we once visited at a place called Teulada at the head of the valley looking down towards Moraira. At first when the estate was being built and marketed there was an attractive swimming pool and a pleasant clubhouse. However, when we paid a return visit about three years later the pool was empty and the clubhouse derelict. There just wasn't the custom to sustain the facilities.

We couldn't see into the future and knew nothing about this on the day of our inspection visit, we just looked around admiring the surroundings.

Antonio was a superb salesman and as we ate he told us about an estate building plot that had just come back onto the market. When the Tabaira development first started, a plot of land could be reserved at a small price with the option of building on the site within a year. If no building work had started within that time, the option lapsed and the plot reverted to the developers. It was one of these plots that Antonio was trying to interest us in.

"Why put up with the restrictions of an apartment when for a little more money you could have the freedom of a villa" he said temptingly, "you could have a 'casa pequena' like the one we saw in the woods at a surprising price." We wondered what he meant by a surprising price. Antonio seemed to have already decided what we were going to have and matters were getting out of control, but in the end we agreed to go and see the plot after finishing our meal.

The vacant plot wasn't too far away at the top of the hill behind the supermarket. The whole area around here was well wooded and the tumbledown remains of ancient terraces, possible Moorish in origin, lay scattered higgledy-piggledy beneath the dense undergrowth. Indeed, the land looked as if it had lain neglected ever since the Moors had left centuries before. Dense thickets of stone oak resembling holly bushes flourished under the canopy of Mediterranean pine trees and the scent of rosemary, wild herbs and pines permeated the air. An ancient carob bean tree thrust out two twisted limbs of bare branches like a tortured human form, with arms stretched out to the sky in agony. Although there was practically no wind, we could swear that the carob bean tree waved its branches at us in greeting. The feature seemed so lifelike that one could almost imagine it coming alive late at night and moving around the domain. In that case we thought if we gave it a trowel it could make itself useful and do some much needed gardening.

The voice of Antonio brought us back to earth. "It is more convenient around here with a south facing aspect and near the supermarket and because the site is on a slope, the hot water cylinder could go under the house. There is plenty of space and we could even build you a swimming pool as well by next August and you could plunge straight in."

"Please stop, Antonio," we replied, "we think we've plunged in far enough already. In fact, I think we're drowning and going down for the third time!"

There is a hidden hazard lurking along the shores of the Mediterranean sea and quite often unsuspecting British holiday makers are at risk. The name of this condition is called Spanish fever and many normally level-headed British people become infected with the virus. The effect of the fever is to cause people to act in strange ways and to make rash decisions. They may experience feelings of supreme confidence and optimism. So what happened next can only be blamed onto Spanish fever, because we decided that we really loved the area and agreed to go the next day to sign a contract at the office of Construcciones Benisa at the nearby town. Having made the decision, it was time to return down the N332 to Benidorm and the free tea at the Playamar.

The town of Benisa is the base of many of the big property developers active along the coast including V.A.P.F. of 'El Cumbre del Sol' fame. The headquarters of Construcciones Benisa turned out to be an impressive modern office block situated at the side of the main road opposite the bus station and a bar/restaurant. Antonio had driven us down from Benidorm again and on arrival, led us into an airy entrance hall where there was a reception desk manned by an expensive looking

An ancient carob bean tree

smartly dressed young women. On each side of the reception area were showrooms containing displays of colourful tiles, marble tops, chrome bathroom fittings, floor coverings and other items of construction for clients to choose from. After a word with the receptionist, Antonio led the way up a wide flight of stairs and through a series of offices where people were at work to the top floor. Eventually we entered a very large room, which seemed to stretch half the length of the building, containing the biggest table we have ever seen. The table was truly immense and would have graced the cabinet room at Number 10 Downing Street. At the far end of the table, as if in the distance, sat a pleasant looking middle-aged Spanish man who smiled at us in greeting. Antonio introduced him as one of the partners in the firm, none other than Senor Pepe, the devastator of the Tabaira lawns. Senor Pepe spoke in Spanish to Antonio, who translated the conversation for us.

"There is some good news and some bad news," said Antonio. "The good news is that the plot of land you are interested in is still available. The bad news is that due to inflation and the high cost of materials, house prices have just risen by twenty percent. However, if you decide to go ahead now your price will only rise by ten percent."

It was perfectly true that inflation was high in Spain at that time and it seemed to us that this was a reputable and old established company. There was even a tale that Franco's widow had shares in the firm and that if there were any kind of a problem with planning permission or building permits, a phone call to Governor of Alicante's office would sort out the matter. "Tell Senor Pepe that it's all right and we'd like to go ahead," we told Antonio, but before signing anything we went for a drink at the café across the main road. This was about the only time that we saw Antonio annoyed. "They didn't tell me anything about this price rise," he fumed, "and I feel like packing it all in and going down to the beach tomorrow." "No, no, please don't do that," we begged him, "you've got a sale and but for you we wouldn't have even heard of Tabaira." We got the distinct impression that somehow our roles had got reversed and that we were the ones now doing the selling. In the end we got him to calm down and we all went back across the road to sign the contract and to pay a deposit. We knew we were taking a

Portet Beach, Moraira

chance and were lucky to avoid possible pitfalls. Quite simply, in Britain a debt follows a person but in Spain it follows the property. Again, it has been rightly said that if something looks too good to be true then it probably is. In one sad case an English lady purchased a villa in Moraira at an unrealistic price from a Dutchman. This man promptly left the country and then it was found that the local bank had a prior mortgage on the property. The English lady couldn't pay the charge, the bank foreclosed and she lost everything. In Britain a new house is usually completed before much money changes hands, but in Spain the payments are made in stages, some when the foundations go in, more when the walls are up and the final payment on completion. To minimise risks it is essential to deal with old-established reputable firms and to use a good lawyer. In the case of the English lady, a simple check at the Land Registry in the town of Denia would have revealed the truth. In our case, our fate was now in the hands of Construcciones Benisa.

THE LEMON EXPRESS

Later in the week there was an excursion advertised on the notice board at the Playamar for a trip on the Lemon Express train, which uses the lines of the trenet. The trenet is the name of the narrow gauge railway that runs up the coast from Alicante. For a time the trains went as far as the town of Gata, but now they only go as far as Denia, a distance of some 93 kilometres. There is a frequent service between Alicante and Benidorm but only a restricted service to the towns further north. The railway line has tunnels and in some places the route follows a succession of cliffs overlooking the sea, giving fine views along the coast.

The British can take some credit for keeping the line open, not only by using the regular service but also by patronising the Lemon Express. This takes its name from the colour of the train's old-fashioned ornate wooden carriages and from the lemon and orange groves passed on the journey. The Lemon Express special train runs from Benidorm to Gata about three times a week and although far from being an 'express' a trip on this train makes an interesting excursion. Our group boarded the excursion bus at the hotel to meet the tour guide waiting at Benidorm's railway station near the market. "Please listen carefully," she said slowly to the group, sounding just like a primary school teacher. "Your coach is 'Carmen' and you must stay with this coach for the whole journey. Please remember to board 'Carmen' on the return trip from Gata."

'Yes, Miss,' we felt like saying. Eileen and I duly boarded 'Carmen' and took our seats at the rear of the coach. A special souvenir was on offer. You could have your name printed on a 'Wanted' poster which depicted a very rough looking wild west desperado with the caption, 'Wanted' for causing alarm and distress on the Lemon Express. Your own name would be printed in large black letters underneath. Orders were set up in type and printed on a hand operated letterpress machine whilst we were visiting Gata. The souvenir offer seemed surprisingly popular and the tour guide took several orders and stuffed the money down the back of her jeans. She sat next to us doing some paper work before leaving to go further up the train. A little later I was surprised to see a thick wad of banknotes lying on the seat beside me, I picked up the notes and looked around. "You keep them" advised a women sitting opposite who had seen what was going on, "they'll only say it's theirs whether they've lost it or not." However, we knew where the notes had come from and returned them to the tour guide who thanked us gratefully.

We duly arrived in Gata and were shepherded into a large garden where slices of tortilla and glasses of sangria were waiting on some tables. "There's plenty for everyone so there's no need to push," said the tour guide and we felt more and more like children. After the sangria and the tortilla we were invited to inspect items of craft and wickerwork for sale and to visit a guitar factory. Some people even bought guitars although I think they had little idea of how to play them.

Then it was time to board 'Carmen' for the return journey and the highlight of the excursion. This was the serving of free 'champagne' (this was before EEC rules about brand products) and the sale of bottles of the same. The 'champagne', if that's what it was, seemed very cheap at only fifty pesetas a bottle, or about half-a-crown in our old currency. We bought two bottles and boldly declared them at the customs on returning to Manchester airport. The customs officer gave the bottles a horrified look and waved us through hastily. Many years later we were waiting for a train at Teulada station near Moraira when there was a whistle in the distance and a train with the same ornate yellow carriages full of waving passengers came round the bend. It was the good old Lemon Express still going strong.

Apart from the Lemon Express the trenet or the 'Rattling Rosie Line' as we nicknamed it from the way the trains rattle along, is a first class introduction to the Costa Blanca. Fares are very cheap and it is possible to visit different resorts en route or to travel all the way to Alicante for a day's outing. The trains run on a daily service of about fifteen journeys in each direction, beginning just after 6a.m. and ending at 11p.m. One day at the end of the holiday having used up all our money, we had to tender a high-value banknote for the fare, having used up all our change. The conductor on the train was an elderly man with a twinkle in his eyes, like a Spanish Mr Pickwick as played by the actor James Hayter. The high-value note seemed to amuse him and he gave the impression that he had never seen such a large sum of money on the train before. "I will have to get more change in Benidorm, Senor," he remarked with a smile. Then humming to himself, he began to play with the note in front of the draughty open carriage window. He first made a paper cup with the note, then a dart and finally a tiny hat, which he pretended to put on his head. We watched in horror expecting all our remaining money to fly out of the window at any second. Finally, when we reached Benidorm he disappeared completely and we thought we'd seen the last of our money. However, on reaching Villajoyosa further down the line the conductor suddenly reappeared like jack-in-the-box with the change, having got on again at the end of the train.

It was as far back as 1864 that a local engineer Jean Batista Lafora had the idea of building a 'small' railway between Alicante and the then rather isolated towns of the northern Costa Blanca. However, after several false dawns, it wasn't until February 13th 1911 that King Alfonso XIII of Spain himself laid the first foundation stone in Villajoyosa. The inaguration of the service between Alicante and Altea took place in 1914, followed by an extension to Denia the following year.

Over the years the railway had many ups and downs, losing freight traffic to road transport in the 1950's. However, in 1968, following a slight increase in passengers, arrangements were made to extend the line from Denia to Gandia making the total length of the railway 123 kilometres. Unfortunately, after four years this new section of the line had to be closed down again. Then on October 14th 1984 came a disaster. An Alicante bound regular train crashed head-on into a northbound special excursion on a single line stretch near Villajoyosa. Ten people died and twenty nine were injured. After the disaster as so often happens the hospitals in Benidorm were overwhelmed with offers help and blood from British people in the resort. Since then a patent French safety system has been installed which eliminates the possibility of any such accident happening again. A few years ago there was a plan to convert the trenet line to standard gauge and extend it to the town of Gandia again, thus linking up with the National network and opening up the entire coast to modern rail travel. But whatever the future holds, this delightful narrow gauge railway is doing quite well for itself at the moment.

The Chicharas (or cicadas) take their name from the sound of the little steam trains that used to chug along local Spanish country railways. Many of these lines are long closed down, but their traces can still be seen in derelict stations, old track beds and broken bridges. One such railway once ran from San Felieu to Gerona on the Costa Brava in the sixties. Unfortunately, the train used to take about three hours for a journey that could be done by car in half an hour. We once took a trip on this train and it was rather uncomfortable and dirty as the engine puffed out thick smoke. But who knows, perhaps with better rolling stock and investment the line could have been saved like the trenet.

The Spanish Parliament first approved the construction of the railway line from Alcoy to the port of Gandia in 1886. However Gandia's Parliamentary representative had to travel to England to find a company capable of meeting the challenge. So it was that an English company became involved and that all the lines and the engines for the railway were made in Birmingham and Manchester. The railway opened in June 1892 and lasted for seventy-six years. Apart from obvious industrial advantages there was an unexpected use that nobody could have imagined. People from Alcoy began to use the train to take outings to the beaches of Gandia, the beginnings of tourism. Over the years the prosperity of the line mirrored Spain's economic progress. However, by 1965 the English company that had developed the line was dissolved and the state took over. The last trip of the Alcoy 'chicharra' took place on April 15th 1969 amidst great emotion. A contemporary photograph shows a group of aficionados holding up a banner reading 'Adios Querido Chicharra' (Goodbye Beloved Chicharra).

It is said that a journey on this railway had a special character of its own. There was plenty of smoke and soot and surprises that wouldn't be looked on so kindly today. Passengers sometimes had to get out whilst the engine worked up enough steam to climb the steepest section of the track! Sometimes passengers even had to alight and gather firewood to stoke up the boiler, a thing that would cause an uproar today, but that was looked on as absolutely normal at the time. The boiler wasn't the only thing needing topping up, because local people supplied jugs of beer to the drivers as the trains passed by. Today, many years later, there are plans to restore the old route into a long distance footpath, a cycle track or an ecological route.

The remains of these old railways are widespread if you look carefully. In Torrevieja the railway only closed fairly recently and the former station has been refurbished and is now a museum cum tourist office. One of the main functions of the railway in the past was the transport of sea salt and there is a display of old railway trucks containing salt near the port. You can now walk or cycle along the bed of the old rail track right around the salt lagoon behind the town and sometimes an old rail or a sleeper can be spotted in the undergrowth. The inland town of Bocairente near Alcoy has a station but no railway. As in other places, the local tourist information office recommends walks following the line of the old railway tracks. Now the wheel has turned full circle and as in Britain, there is talk of trying to re-instate some of these old railways again.

Club Tabaira

EARLY DAYS

All this happened in the late nineteen seventies before the coming Spanish property boom. Antonio had sent us a photograph and a progress report about the latest situation and by the following Christmas Construcciones Benisa had built a small 'El Nid' (the nest) type villa on the chosen area. Antonio had told us that this was the last 'El Nid' type to be built on an 800 square metre plot. In future, any newly built villas would be bigger and more expensive.

In an idealistic notion of natural conservation we had instructed the builders to leave as many trees standing as possible, a mistake that would haunt us for years to come. After the builders departure we left with a dense jungle of vegetation growing beneath the canopy of adult pines that hemmed in the house. There were flourishing thickets of stone oak with their sharp holly like leaves and tough tenacious roots, colonies of prickly furze and clumps of rosemary and thyme, which have useful culinary uses. Other plants like sedum, wild lilies, canes, a kind of wiry grass and weeds of all kinds were growing in rampant profusion all around.

The situation would have made a fine subject for a B.B.C. television gardening programme, a kind of Spanish 'Lost Gardens of Heligan' to transform and regenerate. Our old friend the ancient carob bean tree was still standing nearby and it seemed to rustle its leaves in greeting when we arrived for the first time. Indeed, it seemed to be in rude health with several plump pods growing from its lower branches. We had heard of an old Spanish saying which roughly translated means in English:-

A Spanish holiday villa

'He who moves a carob bean tree
'All day and night shall wail and moan in misery.'

Not wishing to suffer a similar fate, we gave orders that the bean tree should be left untouched and we planned to make it a feature of the garden.

Luckily, Antonio helped us to get established and he did far more for us than one could expect with advice on buying furniture and paying bills, so that in the end we came to think of him as being more of a friend than a business acquaintance. He took us into Benisa to buy some heavy duty Spanish agricultural hoes, unlike anything seen in Britain and marched triumphantly round the Plaza Mayor with the implements on his shoulder, much to the merriment of the locals who imagined he'd gone back to farming. With the aid of these tools more suited to local conditions we began to make some inroads on the jungle around the house.

Our nearest neighbours Hans and Mia were a retired Dutch couple who lived in a villa just across the road. Hans suffered from a bronchitic health condition and as a consequence the couple spent lengthy periods in Spain during the winter months. It wasn't long before Hans made himself known. He had a habit of watching us when we were working in the front garden and offering what he imagined was helpful advice.

"You are working well," was his favourite opening gambit.

"Thank you, Hans," we would reply. "We have to keep up with the Mullers."

"I see you are planting some cypress trees," continued Hans, "I would put them near the gate where they can be seen."

"Thanks for your advice Hans, that's just what we were going to do."

We felt like playing an unkind trick on him as in recent Maxwell House coffee advertisement. In the advert some British people are drinking some coffee when they are approached by a Continental friend called Hans.

'I see that you are having coffee,' enquires the friend, eyeing the cups hopefully, and 'there is enough for three, ja?'

'You're absolutely right, Hans,' the British reply and promptly drink up all the coffee themselves.

At the beginning the little house was overshadowed and darkened by the encroaching woods, including one large pine tree that we nicknamed 'Old Sequoia' after the giant redwood trees of southern California. 'Old Sequoia' was growing far too near the house, its roots were undermining the foundations and it was taking up all the sunshine and light. The big tree would have to go, but the attempt to get rid of it almost destroyed the casa pequena before we'd hardly started to use it. Through Hans we made the acquaintance of a local builder named Miguel, who arranged for what he called some 'expert foresters' to come and help us cut down 'Old Sequoia'. One afternoon a few days later a battered dusty van drew up with a screech of brakes on the road outside. Two Spanish workmen jumped out of the van and we guessed that they must be the 'expert foresters' that we had been expecting. They seemed in a great hurry to get started and didn't bother with any preparatory work. We imagined that they would have come prepared with ropes to steady the heavy trunk and guide it away from the house in a safe direction. However, there were no ropes and we began to suspect that our so-called 'experts' were doing the job on the side and had lingered rather too long in the local bar.

After sizing up 'Old Sequoia' for a minute or two, one of the men proceeded to shin straight up the tree-trunk to the topmost branches with the agility of a coconut monkey. We were suitably impressed, but not with what happened next, because getting out an axe, the man began to lop branches off the tree. Some of these branches were quite heavy and falling from a height, crashed down on the roof, breaking some of the terra-cotta tiles. We shouted at him in our limited Spanish "mas despacio" (slower) and "no dano" (no damage) and he began to work more carefully. After devastating the tree for a few more minutes the man came down to earth again, skipping from branch to branch as quickly as he had gone up. Then, returning to the back of the battered van, the men got out a dangerous looking motorised chain saw.

They started up the saw and began to work at the base of the pine making two sloping cuts at each side of the trunk, one above the other. The smell of resin filled the air and sawdust flew in all directions. This went on for several minutes until, apparently satisfied with their efforts, the men stopped work and stood well back, obviously expecting developments. However, 'Old Sequoia' wasn't going to give in without a fight and refused to fall. The men waited another minute or two but nothing happened, they scratched their heads, looked puzzled and then started up the chain saw again and renewed their assault on the base of the trunk. Just then a strong gust of wind caught the top-most branches of the pine tree. There was a horrific crack, the men jumped back as if stung and the whole tree started to topple majestically as if in slow motion. The men had miscalculated their cut, but there was nothing in the world anyone could do to stop it as the giant trunk slewed sideways, lodging itself on the branches of an adjacent pine and partially overhanging the roof of the house.

"This is it," I said to Eileen, "everything's being going too well for us so far and now our luck's running out." We held our breath for a few seconds, which seemed like an eternity. Suddenly there was a second frightful crack as the supporting branch on the neighbouring pine suddenly broke and as if by a miracle the immense carcass of 'Old Sequoia' swung out wide and fell with a sickening crunch amidst clouds of dust just inches outside the porch. Our good luck was still holding out.

As the dust settled one of the 'expert foresters' looked at us with a sheepish grin and mumbled an apologetic sounding 'muy bien' (very good). "Don't answer him," advised Hans who had come out to see the pantomime. It was only by good luck that the tree hadn't fallen across the roof and destroyed the house and we agreed that the whole performance had been 'muy malo' (very bad). Finally, the men used chains to drag the heavy trunk to the edge of the road because the wood was valuable. A few days later the trunk disappeared and that was the last we saw of our giant pine, except that its stump somehow didn't rot and the remains were still visible at the side of the house for years afterwards.

Tall slender cypress pines add a contrast of shape and colour to a Mediterranean garden. Unlike the pines, the cypress trees are completely harmless because their roots grow into a ball and don't invade nearby drains or damage house foundations. There is a quaint custom in Provence in southern France concerning cypress trees described by Lady Fortescue in her charming book 'Perfume from Provence'. When a new owner takes possession of a house, two special symbolic cypress trees named 'peace' and 'prosperity' are planted in the garden. Accordingly, Lady Fortescue planted two trees in her garden when she took possession, but noted that the tree named 'peace' got badly nipped by the frost. Her local gardener old Hilaire explained that this was because 'La Paz' (peace) never prospered as well as its brother because there was no peace in the world. "Very true" remarked Lady Fortescue, but she was surprised that even cypress trees knew this painful truth. Eileen and I were impressed by this story and decided to try the same thing ourselves, planting two cypress trees at each side of the front drive. Unfortunately both trees promptly died and it was clear that we were not going to enjoy peace and prosperity just yet. It wasn't until we had a second attempt, planting two more trees at the back of the house, that the cypresses started to prosper.

Over the years we fought something of a losing battle with the pine trees. If we cut down any saplings the adult trees the grew much more and were expensive to get rid of. One February we arrived in Tabaira to be greeted enthusiastically by Hans. This was out of character for him and we wondered what he really wanted. "You have come at the right time, we are attacking the caterpillars," announced Hans, as if it was some kind of military operation. "I will take you down the hill to get the lopper from Oscar." The lopper consisted of a long pole with an arrangement of cords controlling heavy shears that would cut off any branches out of normal reach. We weren't too thrilled about this, not wishing to spend our precious time in Spain killing caterpillars.

During the winter months nest-like objects appear on the pine trees, hanging from their branches like Christmas decorations. These nest-like constructions contain the eggs of the Mediterranean processionary pine caterpillar. In spring with the warmer weather the eggs begin to hatch out, the nests burst and the grubs emerge. For some reason the caterpillars seem bent on locating to pastures new and lines of the creatures can seen moving in single file around gardens or crossing roads. Normally the birds would eat these caterpillars, but they are protected toxic dust, which coats their hairy bodies and impregnates their nests. This dust is dangerous to humans and can give a nasty rash or worse if touched; one of our neighbours was bedridden for days after contact with the substance. So using Oscar's lopper, we cut the nests off our pine trees carefully, standing well clear to avoid the dust. Then after pushing the nests together, we set fire to them and watched them burn from a safe distance. After doing this we felt we had fulfilled our civic duty and returned the lopper to Oscar.

Oscar who lent us the lopper was another acquintance who helped us in our early days at Tabaira. He was Austrian, very tall with a commanding presence, had a loud voice and lived with his wife Rosie in a villa not far away down the steep hill on the way to Moraira. The villa had been one of the first to be built on the urbanisation, enjoyed a prime position with views of Moraira towards the sea and boasted a large garden planted with almond and citrus trees. Oscar had been a successful film producer in the past, specialising in documentaries about African wild life and his villa was filled with native artefacts such as shields, spears, masks and carved wooden objects. Unfortunately,

The road to Moraire many yars ago

during his years in Africa he had picked up a nasty health condition called Bilharzia, a minute parasite of the blood which troubled him and for which he still received treatment.

Around this time plant thieves who used to steal attractive plants and shrubs from villa gardens whilst the owners were away had plagued the district. One day Oscar ambushed this gang of plant thieves and gave them the fright of their lives. Oscar was relaxing on the patio in front of the villa one sunny afternoon when he heard the sound of a car drawing up on the hill outside next to his garden. The car doors opened and excited German voices were heard at the sight of the healthy fruit trees growing below. Cries of "mandel, mandel" (spade) were heard as the Germans climbed over the garden fence and began to dig around the base of a lemon tree. Suddenly, Oscar rose to his full height on the patio above and boomed out in his loudest film-directors voice. "What do you think you are doing? Why are you digging in my garden? Get out the lot of you!" The effect was electric. The Germans stopped digging as if paralysed, then dropping their spades where they were they jumped back over the fence and fled pell-

Teulade Station, Spain, November 1986

mell down the hill in blind panic as fast as they could run and there was no need of a flight of African spears to speed them on there way.

"Come back, come back," boomed Oscar, "I don't want your car leaving there," but the Germans had fled out of sight. The abandoned car disappeared in the middle of the night, but the plant thefts stopped after this.

Moraira, Costa Blanca

EATING OUT

Every weekend in England our local evening paper features a good food column ostensibly written by a person named Oliver. I always imagine Oliver as being a prosperous looking middle aged businessman with expensive tastes, who seems to be carrying on a clandestine love affair with a mysterious 'guest' or 'companion' who accompanies him to the different restaurants. In actual fact I don't suppose that Oliver really exists, but that the name is in reality the 'nom de plume' of any of the journalists that the paper sends out each week. There seems to be a number of similar imaginary characters in today's business and advertising worlds. Is there a real life Alison Dale who writes 'personal' letters to the customers of the Damart clothing company, or a genuine Tom Champagne whose signature appears on the impressive documents sent out by the Readers Digest magazine, which congratulate you for reaching the third stage of the competition (for the umpteenth time)?

These good food guides and articles are widespread in many local newspapers and magazines and are written under various names like Oliver, Falstaff or Benedict. I imagine that if printing had been invented at the time, even Friar Tuck would have penned some kind of eating out guide for 'Ye Sherwood Forest Herald' describing meals served up at Loxley Hall or at Nottingham Castle.

'On Wednesday evening my companion and I dined out in the banqueting hall at Nottingham Castle. From a varied menu I chose the Sheriff of Nottingham's special, the spit-roasted wild boar with apple, which was succulent and done to a turn. My companion Maid Marion sampled the local forest venison with herbs, which she declared delicious. The meal was accompanied with a flagon of pleasant mead produced by the monks of nearby Newstead Abbey and at only ten groats we thought the bill very reasonable. Friar Tuck.'

The good food guide in our local English paper entitled 'Eating Out with Oliver' is written in an expansive style that assumes that its readers, if not millionaires are at least very prosperous and that money is no object. The restaurants selected for review often have fashionable foreign names and are awarded a maximum of five stars in different categories like food, service, atmosphere and value. Eileen and I read these reports with amusement, marvelling at the exorbitant prices and thinking that it would be possible to feed a family for a week on the same amount of money. In Spain, the local English language newspaper the 'Costa Blanca News' carries a similar eating out guide and with literally hundreds of restaurants between Benidorm and Moraira there is plenty of choice to review. In spite of all this choice, your friends and acquaintances always seem to know of one special restaurant, which they say, is unique and they insist on taking you there.

"We must go to the Gaviota restaurant, no-one knows about it yet and it's tremendous value."

The restaurant in question sported an old-fashioned handcart on its roof as an advertisement and for years we thought that the word 'gaviota' meant a handcart. It was only years later that we discovered that the real meaning of the word was a seagull.

Although we only saw her occasionally when our visits co-incided, a near neighbour Pauline was another good friend. She lived next door to Hans further down the hill, was middle-aged and had teen-aged children and we met her shortly after our arrival at Tabaira. Nothing seemed to upset Pauline, she took every crisis in her stride and was a master of the understatement. She was 'quite annoyed' when she found out that her villa had been built facing in the wrong direction and 'rather vexed' when her hire car broke down on the way back to the airport. One day in June when we didn't have a car she invited three of us to go out for a meal at a restaurant near the nearby town of Javea.

"I'd like to take you to this restaurant because it specialises in rural cooking" Pauline explained.

We drove out of Moraira along the Javea road, passing the golf course at Benitachell and eventually arrived at this 'rural' restaurant under the shadow of the Mongo mountain. As it was a warm day we decided to sit outside on some benches at a bare wooden trestle table, with scenic views all around. We ordered the meal and after a time a large leg of lamb, roasted with local herbs, arrived on a platter at the table together with some plates and a knife and fork wrapped in a serviette for each person. Accompanying all this was a large barra of bread, evidently we were expected to tear chunks of bread from the barra with our bare hands while we ate, an integral part of the 'rural' cuisine we had come to experience. Although the lamb was delicious, everything seemed a bit basic and I imagined it must have been something like this at a peasants' banquet in medieval times with only a jousting tournament to complete the scene.

As we ate Pauline pointed out a large luxury villa standing on a distant hillside.

"You see that villa below those pine trees" she said. "The one that looks as if it belongs to the Governor of Alicante," we replied.

"It's actually owned by an Englishman who used to work in the Far East, he came out here and bought that luxury villa when he retired, now he's complaining that some Chinese people are threatening him for some reason. He is grumbling that his only protection is a pet Alsatian dog." We wondered why the Chinese were threatening him, perhaps he'd fallen out with the local Dragon City restaurant? It has been said that the Chinese will eat anything on four legs, so we hoped they wouldn't kidnap the pet Alsatian dog and serve it up with bean sprouts as a revenge.

All this time I noticed that an inconspicuous looking man sitting at the next table had been taking a great deal of interest in our conversation. As we talked he turned his head and leaned in our direction, obviously trying to hear what we were saying. I tried to think who he could be, perhaps he was a tabloid newspaper reporter or even a government treasury spy. It was all very interesting.

Pauline seemed to have a liking for unusual restaurants and on another occasion she took us to a place inland along the road to the town of Gata called the 'Tasca on the Brow' (the Pub on the Brow), which specialised on meats cooked on the 'inferno'. The inferno turned out to be a large bonfire that suddenly flared up in a frightening way and singed the food that was being cooked. The Tasca had a thatched roof, which given the proximity of the inferno was something of a fire hazard and instead of central heating, on cold winter days old-fashioned Spanish charcoal heaters were placed under the tables to warm the diners. The walls and niches around the restaurant were adorned with various items of old junk, faded oil paintings and antiquities that were all for sale. The place became quite dark and shadowy in the evening and if anything was to fall out of the exposed thatched roof I am sure it wouldn't be noticed. A meal here could last at least four hours, which seems fairly common in Spain. On arrival there is a warm welcome and orders are quickly taken, the drinks and the main course soon come, but then the waiters seem to lose interest in your table. As for the bill, it can take almost as long as the meal to arrive and has to be literally prised out of the waiter.

Some of the best restaurants in the province of Alicante are situated inland or in the sierras behind the coast. Just past the town of Benisa, where we went with Antonio to sign the building contract, a right turn off the main N322 takes you along a road leading towards the mountains. At first this road crosses over the north-south autopista and then wends its way across a landscape of barren scrub-encrusted hills. Suddenly the whole Jalon valley is revealed in all its glory like a giant amphitheatre, a veritable Shangri-la surrounded by sheltering mountains. The soil here is extremely fertile and rows of healthy looking vines stretch away into the distance. In the autumn the contrasting colours of the red soil, green leaves and purple grapes make a vivid spectacle. Years ago the grapes from these vines supported an important raisin trade at nearby Denia, with strong British connections. Some old drying sheds or 'riurau' can still be seen; the ripe grapes were dried on wicker frames, which were placed outside the riuraus on south facing patios. If rain threatened the frames could be moved inside the sheds quickly. Today the grapes go to the wine co-operative at Jalon to be made into vast quantities of strong, mostly red wine. Apart from the wine-co-operative the town of Jalon has a Sunday market and is noted for its local honey and the production of mustard.

From here the road continues up the valley and crosses the sometimes-dry Rio Jalon by a bridge with battered guardrails. The next town along the valley is Alcalali, that is famous throughout the the region for its quality restaurants. We once had lunch at a restaurant in Alcalali one rainy Sunday in June. It was the feast of Corpus Christi and there seemed to be a party in progress at the restaurant. Because it was a fiesta the Spanish families were out in force although funnily enough they all seemed to be having steak and kidney pie or roast beef and Yorkshire pudding whilst the British were trying local dishes like paella or olleta, a kind of stew.

After Alcalali the route divides, one road continuing up the valley to the secluded hill town of Castell de Castells and the other one gradually climbing into the mountains towards the pass of the Coll de Rates. It was this road that we usually took and at first there are groves of sweet scented orange and lemon trees, resplendent with their golden globes of ripening fruit. Then there is a belt of shady pinewoods before beginning the ascent towards the summit of the pass. The road climbs steadily with little opposing traffic apart from an occasional convoy of jeep-like open-top vehicles doing the mountain run from Benidorm. At last, with a final hair-pin bend you arrive at the summit of the pass and the Merendero of the Coll de Rates. The word 'merendero' in Spanish means a lunch, snack or picnic spot and it was here that we once enjoyed a simple meal of paella that beat anything we have ever had for sheer value. The Merendero had great character with rough hewn ceiling beams, an open fireplace with a huge cast-iron stove. In those days everything was cooked on charcoal, there was no power or electric light and the place closed at sunset. As we were leaving the Merendero we noticed some unfortunate rabbits being slaughtered behind the kitchen for the next days paella. This took place many years ago and unfortunately things change so things could be different now.

After passing the Merendero the road descends from the pass through a most beautiful landscape of secluded valleys and isolated orchards connected by rough tracks. All this scenery cradled by vivid ochre coloured peaks outlined against the brilliant blue sky. The next village round here of Tarbena is noted for its delicious sausages

An old wine-press

(embutidos) made from a secret recipe and for the famous Casa Pinet which was one of the most tourist frequented restaurants on the Costa Blanca. The Casa Pinet and its one-handed owner have won many awards from the Department of Tourism and leisure organisations for enterprise and the quality of its food. The place achieved success partly through its excellent cuisine and reasonable prices but also by adopting a 'tongue in cheek' communist/republican theme for the restaurant. Left wing posters and republican slogans decorate the walls and even the bottles of local Tarbena wine had labels displaying the hammer and sickle. The restaurant was featured in the 'Floyd in Spain' television programme around 1993 when Floyd used the location to prepare a meal of fideusa, which is similar to paella but with pasta noodles being used instead of rice. As far as I know the restaurant continues to enjoy success and was very popular with the British.

Back on the coast at Moraira our own favourite restaurant and tapas bar used to be a place called the 'Cap d'Or,' conveniently situated opposite the harbour, before the yacht marina was built in the early nineties. We became friendly with the local family who ran this bar which was something of a social meeting place. We used to see Antonio in the tapas bar here after Construcciones Benisa opened an office for a subsidiary firm called Cavipco. Eileen and I enjoyed the hospitality of the Cap d'Or for several years during our early times in Moraira. Sadly, nothing goes on forever. "See you next time," we used to say to the family at the end of each visit until one day we returned to find that a new management had taken over and that everything was different. Our friends had sold out, but they still live and work in Moraira and we see them around the village occasionally.

Nature reserve at Torrevieja

THE CASA PEQUENA

Spain turned out to full of different surprises. We arrived for a visit one Easter to find what appeared to be a bundle of rags lying on the porch. "Look at this," I protested to Eileen, "someone has thrown this rubbish over the wall onto our porch." "Put it straight into the dustbin," she replied.

On closer inspection the bundle of rags turned out to be a pair of ladies trousers that had obviously been lying there for some time. I picked up the trousers gingerly to put them in the dustbin when a coin dropped out of one of the pockets.

"What's this," I called to Eileen, "there's some money in these trousers." A closer examination of the trousers revealed more coins and several high value banknotes. How these trousers with money in their pockets came to be lying on our porch was a complete mystery, no rational explanation seemed to make sense. We knew that our neighbour's dog Coffee used to carry off any shoes left outside a villa to his haunts behind the supermarket. However, if he had pulled the trousers off a clothes line, why was money still in the pockets and why hadn't the owner come looking for the garment which was in full view from the road? In the same way, if the trousers had been stolen on the beach, why was the money still there? We asked our neighbour Hermy, who looked after Coffee, if she could throw any light onto the mystery. "Oh yes." She replied, "those clothes have been there for some time, we thought that you had put them there yourselves to stop rainwater getting under the front door." This left us in something of a quandary. We didn't want to get involved with the Civil Guard if we reported the incident. So as the trousers had been there a considerable time, we decided that the best thing to do was to keep the money and to leave it at that.

Eileen and I soon found out that some of the best plants for growing in the garden or in containers around the patio were the various kinds of yuccas, cacti, succulents and agaves that can survive in the wild. No special cultivation seems necessary with plants of this kind and any cuttings will grow if they are simply stuck in the sand or the soil. There is no need to buy these plants as some are to be found growing wild or discarded at the roadside. However, care should be taken when dealing with this triffid like vegetation and always wear glasses when pruning yuccas because their leaves are sharp as swords. We were strolling in the municipal park one day when we spotted an attractive looking cactus covered in what appeared to be fur or cotton wool. A number of shoots were scattered around the base of the cactus where they had dropped off the main stem. "Look at this," I said to Eileen, "We could take some shoots for ourselves." I bent down to pick up the innocent looking shoots when I felt a sharp pain in my hand. My fingers were covered in tiny prickles, which had penetrated the skin, and it took ages to pull out the tiny tenacious spikes. It wasn't surprising that the cactus had been left severely alone.

When walking through the woods we occasionally came across an interesting cactus or a yucca growing wild in the woods suitable for collecting, but sometimes things aren't always what they seem. On one of our jaunts we had spotted an attractive looking yucca growing deep in the woods and returned later with a sharp knife to take a cutting. I was sawing away merrily at the stem of the yucca when plaintive wails of protest were heard coming from the distance.

"Oh dear! You are sawing at our best yucca, we planted it there ourselves. You are ruining our views."

The voices came from a Swedish couple sitting in front of a villa just visible through the trees. The land wasn't theirs, but they had planted yuccas and cacti in the wilderness in an attempt to improve the outlook from their terrace. We looked around more closely and saw that indeed a rudimentary attempt had indeed been made to create a garden. We apologised to the Swedish couple who were very pleasant, but unfortunately the stem of the best yucca had been sawn clean through and the plant toppled over in a drunken manner. We hastily propped up the best yucca in the soil somehow, hoping it would take root again, and beat a quick retreat.

In addition to the plants and shrubs, the garden around the Casa Pequena contained an abundance of wildlife. There were lizards, geckos, tiny grass snakes, snuffling hedgehogs and once a large green snake which side-winded off into the undergrowth at a surprising speed. We once saw a light that looked as if someone had thrown a cigarette over the wall, but which on closer inspection turned out to be a glow-worm. A thunderstorm or an unexpected shower of rain would bring out toads and frogs living under rocks in the garden although we never saw an alacran or Spanish scorpion which can bite just as painfully as their brothers. It is said that there are seven or eight different kinds of snake in Spain, none of these snakes are venomous but some can give a nasty bite if provoked.

On one occasion we had a little gecko living behind a bookcase inside the house. The gecko would appear in the evening hanging onto the wall or the ceiling by its suction-pad like feet. It used to remain motionless for minutes on end until suddenly disappearing into nowhere like magic. I thought the creature would be happier living in the porch and grabbed it to put it outside when unfortunately its tail fell off. This was its defence mechanism to stop it being eaten by a predator. Luckily, it took up residence behind a light fitting in the porch where there were plenty of flying insects and eventually grew another tail.

A house situated in the woods sometimes has an unwelcome guest. The first time we met this pest was when two friends Barbara and Pam who had been staying at the casa pequena returned home and reported hearing a peculiar ticking noise coming from the coffee table. On investigation they discovered what looked like bullet holes on the underside of the table. Being on the point of leaving and not knowing what to do they poured some bleach down the holes and turned the table upside down. However, when we arrived ourselves a short time later the creature was still in fine fettle, ticking away merrily inside the table like a deranged alarm clock and leaving evidence of its presence in the form of fine wood dust. This is how we first made the aquaintance of the Carcoma or the Spanish furniture beetle. We had come prepared with a tin of Rentokil and doused the table with this and some local chemicals. We then isolated the table in a plastic sack under the house and after a time the table seemed to be clear of danger with no sign of activity. We were lucky to save the table because the Carcoma attacks anything made of wood and some people have been known to burn all affected furniture because of the danger of infestation.

One advantage of the casa pequena was that it was easy to maintain. Unfortunately, every so often a sandstorm blowing in from Africa discoloured facing walls, making repainting necessary. When this happened we used waterproof plastic paint and long-handled rollers to re-whiten the walls. What is called 'Cal' is cheaper but needs careful handling because it is really slaked lime, is corrosive and can burn the skin. The lime is put into metal drum, water is added carefully and the mixture is left overnight. We once heard of a man who tried to make some Cal in a plastic drum and the mixture dissolved the container! The Spanish themselves are experts at using Cal, applying it with surprising speed and skill using long bamboo brushes and achieving excellent results.

Because the house was situated on a corner we knew that a wall would be needed. People were starting to use our garden as a short cut in our absence, even coming through when we were in residence. The choice of material for a wall rested between blocks or stone, a block wall costing less than stone but needing more maintenance. The Spanish craftsmen who build these stonewalls are extremely skilled and know exactly which size of stone to select for their work. A parallel could be drawn with the dry stone walling in the Yorkshire Dales. The top of the wall is usually finished off with a layer of cement and a line of decorative blocks added.

Sometime during the early nineties we built a short flight of steps going down to the lower garden. As we mixed the concrete we had the idea of burying a time capsule under the foundations of the steps. With this object in mind we obtained a large glass container and filled it with souvenirs like coins, stamps, a cassette and a newspaper. Packing these objects into the bottle and wrapping everything up in a plastic sheet we buried the time capsule in concrete beneath the second step. Perhaps sometime in the distant future the capsule will be discovered and someone will wonder about the people who lived here in the last quarter of the twentieth century.

Our favourite time in Spain used to be in the autumn after the summer heat had abated, although it could get chilly in the evening after the sun had gone down. One autumn day when the weather was getting cooler I said to Eileen. "Why don't we use the fireplace and enjoy a warm log fire this evening, there's so much wood around here it's a shame not to use it."

"A good idea," agreed Eileen, "we'll buy a grate from Pedro at the ferreteria (hardware shop) around the corner in Tabaira." Pedro was the local Spanish plumber and his wife ran the nearby hardware shop, which was packed full with lots of different items like an Aladdin's cave. Later that day we laid the fire in the grate and stacked pine logs on the hearth in anticipation of a cosy evening. We put a match to the fire and at first it burned well. The pine logs crackled cheerfully, but then choking smoke filled the room and we started coughing. The chimney obviously wasn't drawing properly.

"Quick, open the doors!" I exclaimed, "I'd rather be cold than suffocate." We opened the doors and the cold air rushed in, but the smoke had penetrated all around the house, even into the bedrooms and the cupboards smelt of smoke for weeks afterwards. We told Antonio about the disaster and he admitted that the fireplace had been put in mainly for decorative purposes.

"You will have to stop up one of the openings at the top of the chimney to get a good draught," he advised us. "I should get a gas fire," he continued, "they are much cleaner and more convenient." This is what we did, but found out later that many people around the area installed Norwegian wood-burning stoves, which had their own special pipe leading up inside the chimney. These stoves appeared to work well and made use of the plentiful supplies of pinewood lying around in the forest.

HOME AND AWAY

Recreational walking is recommended as a healthy activity for people of all ages. Of course, there are different levels of fitness according to your circumstances and age. Some people can walk for miles over rough or steep terrain, whilst others can only manage shortish, easy rambles over level routes and we come into this category.

Eileen and I once helped to organise a walking group of friends for easy countryside outings in Yorkshire. We used to survey the walks in advance and preferred facilities like car parks, picnic areas, toilets, way marking and nature trails. Our group should have been called the 'Nothing too Strenuous' or the 'Hit or Miss Walkers' because attendances could vary so wildly. We used to get the best support when there were no popular football matches, school sports or social events taking place on the same day. Of course, good weather helped, which is something you can't control and we were always anxious about this the week before a walk. Surprisingly it can be too warm for walking, even in England. When leading a walk it's a good idea to carry several maps and an orienteering compass which seems to impress people. Also, it's wise to remember 'Murphy's Law' that if something can go wrong it will do and to be absolutely clear about all relevant details and instructions. If you specify meeting at the riverside car-park, you could find out on the day that there are actually two car-parks, one on each side of the river. When some of the expected members fail to arrive you have to search around, driving frantically from one car-park to another to round up the flock. Then there are reproachful comments like, "You did say the riverside carpark." Another problem is that some people

Costa Blanca - North

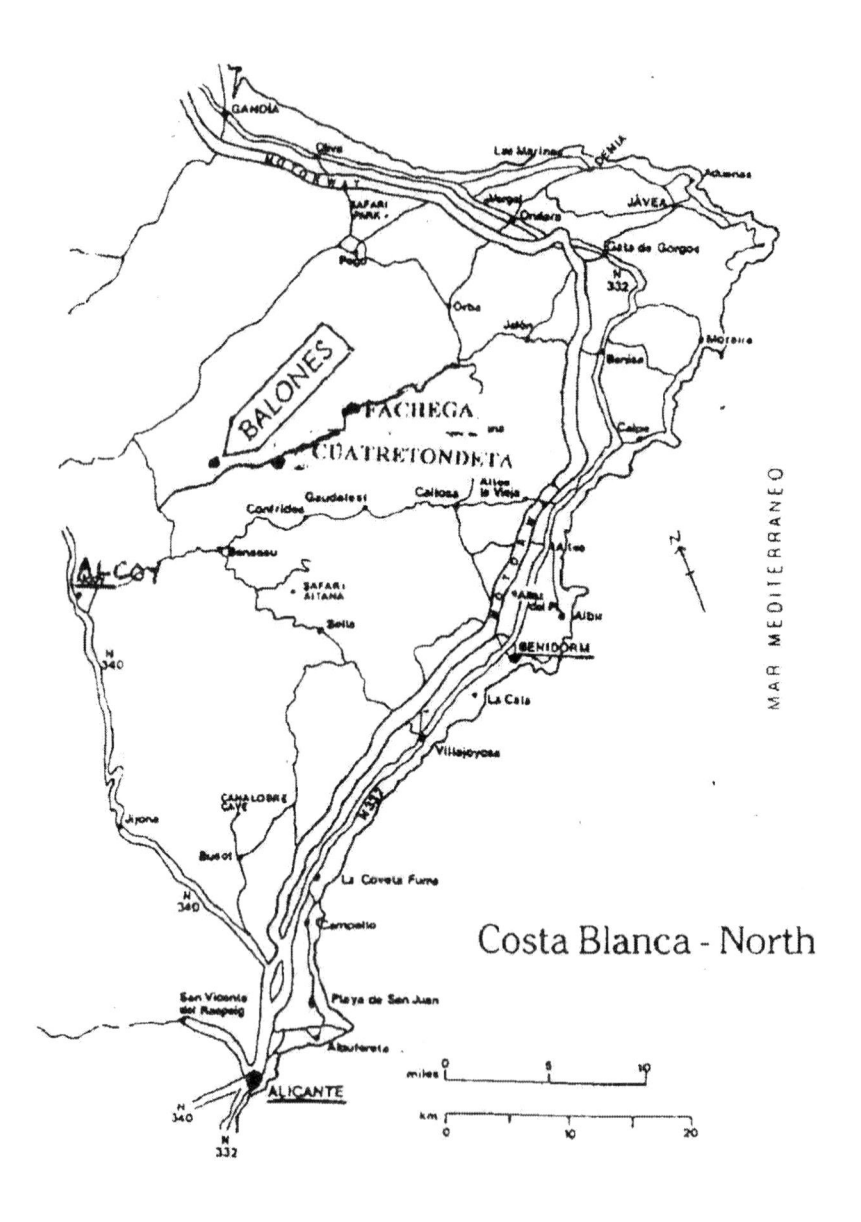

seem to have a very poor sense of direction, will misinterpret the clearest instructions and blame you. "We're late because we missed the turn off the main road, your instructions weren't clear!"

One July we advertised what we imagined would be the best walk of the season and one that we hoped would attract good support. This was the Shawl Walk at Leyburn in Wensleydale in north Yorkshire. This walk takes its name from a supposed historical incident when Mary Queen of Scots, attempting to escape from nearby Bolton Castle, dropped her shawl on this path near Leyburn. The shawl must have been found and recognised by pursuers because history tells us that the wretched Queen was caught and taken back to the Castle, to face more years of captivity and eventual execution.

We were blessed with good weather as our small group waited in Leyburn Market Place at the appointed time. Suddenly there was a commotion in the distance with a loud barking noise and one of our members appeared, being dragged along by a large golden retriever dog. The dog seemed to be very boisterous and hard to manage and we felt sorry for our friend Eddy who had given the creature and its mistress a lift from Moortown in Leeds. The dog called Benjy, had a nose lead instead of one from its collar in an attempt to curb its exuberance because as we found out, a few months earlier it had pulled its mistress off her feet in the park and she had broken her ankle. Disappointingly, no-one else arrived after this, so we decided to make a start, following a lane out of the top of the Market Place to the right of the Bolton Arms and taking it in turns to be towed along by the dog. The Shawl walk follows a high-level track along the limestone escarpment above the valley, which offers fine views down Wensleydale with the looming mass of Penhill opposite. Benjy didn't seem to be very used to the countryside because at the first field he made a series of strong lunges towards some distant sheep, which he seemed to think were other dogs. At first, the path along the escarpment was easy and smooth underfoot, but then we came to a stile as the route descended through some fields to the valley bottom. To get over the stile it was necessary to lift the dog, which weighed almost as much as an adult person, and manhandle it across the top bar. Naturally, Benjy didn't like this treatment and struggled frantically to get free. I don't think that we could have overcome this obstacle without the help of a passing walker, who must have thought that it was his unlucky day. It took three of us all our efforts to lift the dog over the stile safely. After crossing the stile it turned out to be a case out of the frying pan and into the fire as we found ourselves in a vast meadow occupied by a herd of cows grazing right across the line of the path. The cows lifted their heads and regarded Benjy suspiciously with their bulging eyeballs. Knowing that dogs and cows don't mix, we hoped that we wouldn't get trampled by maddened cattle as, with Benjy on a short lead, we gingerly threaded our way through the herd. After this there were no more incidents as our route passed the village of Preston-under-Scar, crossed the Wensleydale railway line and reached the river Ure for what the guide book described as an idyllic, tranquil stretch of path alongside the river bank. As we approached the river, Benjy saw the water and there was no holding him as he made a sudden irresistible bound down the river bank and plunged 'Whoosh' straight into the river like a water splash ride at a theme park, dragging me into the shallows behind him. The dog drank his fill and wallowed in the cool water of the muddy river bed before returning to the bank and shaking himself energetically. We managed to get Benjy under control again, but he was already beginning to smell under the warm sun and we felt sorry for Eddy in the car on the way home.

In Spain, the local English language newspaper the 'Costa Blanca News' carries information about the many different activities taking place up and down the coast. One October, Eileen and I noticed that an organisation named the Costa Blanca Mountain Walkers were holding an event at a village called Fachega some miles inland near the town of Alcoy. We telephoned the contact number given in the paper for details and were warned to allow plenty of time for the journey to the village because the mountainous approach roads were difficult to negotiate with lots of hairpin bends. In fact, these roads up in the mountains turned out to be newly surfaced, well graded, practically deserted and a joy to drive on. One suspects that a large amount of E.E.C. cash had paid for these road improvements with Britain making a substantial contribution.

You couldn't mistake the starting point at the bar in Fachega because of the number of large expensive cars parked outside and a prominent folding bill-board with an arrow and a sign reading 'Mountain Walkers' this way in bold letters. The group was obviously well organised and we bought a programme for two hundred pesetas (this was before the euro) the sole condition for joining the walk. In the programme we noticed that all the walks were graded according to difficulty, starting with an A grade signifying easy going on good tracks through to an X grade for extra challenging. There didn't seem to be too many A grades on the list and in fact the walk we were doing now was an SC grade, which was the second hardest grade and stood for 'strenuous, mostly rough walking' and we wondered what we were letting ourselves in for.

When everyone was ready, the group of over thirty set off in brilliant sunshine along a level farm track passing the fruitful olive and almond groves of this lovely upland valley. Everything seemed to be going fine for the first twenty minutes as we strode out easily along the track and our spirits began to rise. Then suddenly the leader struck off towards the left up a very steep scree-covered slope, which we had to climb in short tiring steps. There was no obvious path on this wild mountainside, but there must have been something marked on the military map that the leader was using. We soon started to struggle, slipping on the loose shale, but we knew that if going up a mountain is hard, coming down is much more difficult. We had decided to turn back when the 'sweeper' of the group approached and advised us kindly, "You won't make it, it's wiser to give up now than to risk an injury. Last month one of our members had to be taken off the mountain by helicopter after breaking an ankle. Today we'll be crossing high ridges and walking along the edges of steep cliffs which can be very demanding. Most of our members are experienced mountaineers and I was a bit doubtful when you only mentioned the Yorkshire Dales before we set off." We had to agree that Otley Chevin was hardly in the same league as the Swiss Alps, so our friend escorted us back down the hill to safe ground and invited us to try one of their easier walks later on. Back at the village half an hour later we scanned the sun-baked sierras to discern the group, now an indistinct blur and barely visible, disappearing over the distant peaks. We hoped they had a good day, but wondered how an X grade walk could be any harder.

Some years later we got involved with another group called the Marina Walkers based near Torrevieja south of Alicante. Our first outing with the Marina Walkers turned out to be a low-level ramble along a nearby seashore, returning through some pinewoods and sand dunes. This group turned out to be just as well organised as the Mountain Walkers when we arrived at the starting point of the walk. Everyone seemed to be very pleasant and welcoming and officials wearing armbands with the words 'Leader' and 'Official' greeted us. An informative programme was given to us containing details about the group and the programme of walks for the current season, including relevant maps. After a time we were startled by a shrill whistle blast signalling the start of the walk and the medium sized crowd trooped off along the sands behind the leader. "There aren't many here today," an official informed us, "it's a bit too near home and everyone knows this area." We walked steadily along the seashore until we reached the mouth of the Rio Segura, when another whistle-blast signalled a rest stop at the halfway stage of the walk. On the return journey through the pinewoods we noticed that people were gathering sticks of windfalls in carrier bags and were told that this was for a group barbecue to be held at the end of the walk. Evidently the group organised social events like barbecues and meals as well as walks. The only problem with the Marina Walkers was that some of their events proved to be a little too popular. On one walk, which was scheduled to finish at a local restaurant near the salt lagoon, forty people had booked a meal, but eighty people turned up on the day, overwhelming facilities.

We stayed with the Marina Walkers for some time, although some of their walks could be quite strenuous and demanding on a par with the Mountain Walkers. We weren't getting any younger, so we selected walks within our capabilities.

Las Naciones Garden

EXPLORING INLAND

The Jalon valley near Benisa, where we signed the contract with Antonio, leads into the heart of the mountains inland on the Costa Blanca. The town of Jalon itself boasts a popular wine co-operative selling mostly strong red wine, a market and pleasant walks beside the usually dry Rio Jalon. In certain seasons the river can be in full flow, at such times beware the gnats of Jalon that can cover you with bites without you realising it! The next town along the valley is Alcalali, noted for its excellent restaurants and their good value. A left turn here leads up to the Coll de Rates pass, the Merendero and the village of Tarbena. Continuing up the valley in the other direction eventually brings you to the mountain town of Castell de Castells. Just past here you arrive at a surprising scene. At first sight there appears to be a crowd of giant hooded monks, the smallest eight metres tall, standing on the slope just below the cliffs at the top of the sierra. In fact, these objects are rock formations created by erosion and wind over the ages. They are known as 'Els Frares' (the Brothers) and the name of the nearby village of Quatretondeta is derived from the tonsure or shaven head worn by the monks.

On the other side of the valley there used to be a small English guesthouse called the 'Casa Serella' run by our friend Demelza who is of Cornish origin. Demelza, her husband and family came out to Spain during the property boom of the late eighties and remained when the market entered one of its periodic recessions later on. Balones itself is a charming old village, which, like many similar places, is built on the slopes of a steep hillside. Although the population of the place is numbered only in hundreds there is a thriving community life with a

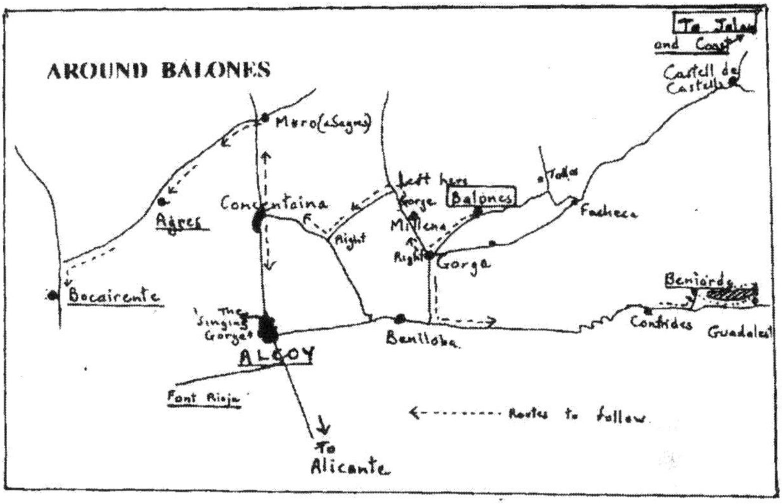
AROUND BALONES
and Coast
Castell de Castells
Concentaina
Agres
Left here
Gorge
Balones
Millena
Right
Right
Gorga
Facheca
Beniardá
Bocairente
The Singing Gorge
ALCOY
Benilloba
Confrides
Guadalest
Font Rioja
Routes to follow
To Alicante

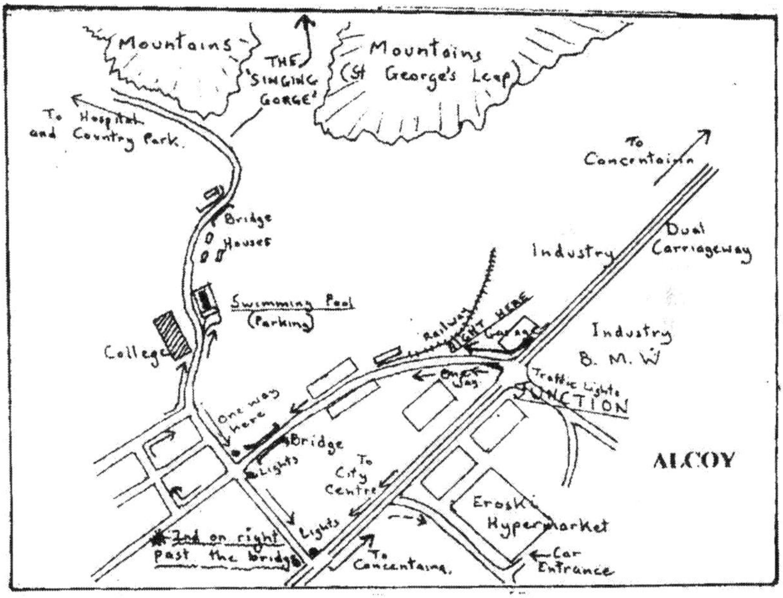
Mountains
THE 'SINGING GORGE'
Mountains (St George's Leap)
To Hospital and Country Park
To Concentaina
Bridge
Houses
Industry
Dual Carriageway
Swimming Pool (Parking)
Railway
RIGHT HERE
Garage
Industry
B. M. W
College
One way
Traffic Lights
JUNCTION
One way here
Bridge
Lights
To City Centre
ALCOY
Eroski Hypermarket
Lights
2nd on right past the bridge
To Concentaina.
Car Entrance

church, a school, a communal swimming pool, a restaurant, bars and even a town hall which is open two or three times a week. We used to visit the 'Casa Serella' occasionally and one dark and windy February evening Demelza took us to see an old village house that was for sale at the time. The old house must have looked the same two hundred years before with its three stories, antique ironwork balconies, decaying wooden beams and walls of immense thickness. There was a great wooden doorway big enough to accommodate a horse and cart, which was its original purpose. Demelza produced a large, clumsy, antique iron key and inserted it into the ancient lock. The wooden doors creaked open ponderously like the lock gates on a canal to reveal a dark cave-like hallway, dimly lit by a swaying bare light bulb that cast dancing shadows around the paint peeling walls To add to the ghostly effect, a moaning wind kept up a chorus of eerie whines and unsettling clattering noises in the upper floors of the ancient building. It was like something out of a book by Edgar Allan Poe and we half expected to find a raven croaking 'Nevermore' behind the door.

Demelza led the way downstairs where she said there was something of interest to see. She told us that it was an old Spanish custom to include the skull of a Moor in the foundations of a house in the belief that it would prevent another Moorish invasion. We stumbled down some uneven steps and arrived in a vast cellar where it would have been possible to entertain whole coach loads of British tourists to a chicken or a pork barbecue. Another dim light bulb swung from the ceiling and tried unsuccessfully to illuminate the area giving more ghostly shadows. But there, just by the wall, there was enough light to make out the rounded shape of a dusty-looking skull, brown with age, set into the cement of the cellar floor. Naturally, just as we saw the skull, an extra loud clattering noise emanated from one of the upper rooms and in the dim light we imagined that it could be the ghost of the Moor coming back for his skull. Our nerves failed and we beat a hasty retreat back upstairs. We hoped that whoever bought the old house would have strong nerves and was not superstitious. The Spanish do seem to have a taste for the macabre and in the cathedral at Barcelona there is a carved Moor's severed head that makes the sound of an organ-pipe when its mouth opens.

Behind Balones

The terrain on this side of the valley at Balones is completely different to the craggy rocks and mountains at Quatretondeta. Over here, well defined tracks meander upwards through orchards of olives, almonds, peaches, cherries, apples and pears to gentle rolling uplands of chalk. From the summit of these uplands above Balones there is a view over to the next valley with a large embalso (dam) way off in the distance. In the other direction the distant mountain ranges are dotted with lonely white villages clinging to the sides of the foothills. It is very quiet and peaceful up here with only the occasional cry of an unseen bird or the distant chimes of a church-bell in the valley below to break the spell. The rays of the setting sun, falling on the rocks of the far away mountain chains, cast strange shadows resembling castles or fanciful palaces that seemed real in the fading light. We walked along the hilltop track until the twilight and it became obvious that more time would be needed to explore any further.

A few miles from Balones the 'Barranco de Sing' or 'Singing Gorge' as it is known is an attraction situated on the northern edge of the town of Alcoy. As you approach Alcoy, bear right off the main road and make for the Municipal Swimming Pool. On our visit the pool was closed for the season, even though it was only early September and the weather was still very warm. However, we talked to the resident attendant who was obviously proud of the facility and delighted to show us around. From the pool you can walk up the road, passing some houses and crossing a bridge, to the obvious entrance of the gorge, which is guarded on each side by two peaks. These are named 'St George's Leap' because it is said that St George, on his horse of course, once leapt from one peak to the other. With a jump like this he would be a runaway favourite to win the Grand National!

The 'Singing Gorge' is a lovely place with high white limestone cliffs on either side and an air of peace and tranquillity broken only by the sound of falling water and the echo of your footsteps. There is a wide variety of plants, flowers and wildlife living in this sheltered gorge. Basking lizards and snakes can be seen sometimes sunning themselves

The 'Singing Gorge' at Alcoy

on rocks near the path whilst glittering dragonflies dart about hunting their prey above pools in the bed of the stream flowing down the gorge. At one point a mountain spring of icy water bubbles from the rocks and we saw a group of Spanish walkers re-filling their water bottles from the pure source. The paths along the gorge are very good and have been reinforced in places with paving stones making for easy walking. The going is level with no dry waterfalls to climb over and we only came across one damp patch on our visit. We only had time to walk part of the way up the gorge, but according to the map the route wends its way through the mountains to the village of Agres, several kilometres further on.

On the other side of Alcoy towards Alicante there is the most magnificent nature reserve in the whole province, the Font Roja. On our first visit I misread the Spanish road signs and ended up in Alcoy itself before I could turn round. Back on the correct route we came to an unsignposted fork and chose to turn left up a narrow road that led to a forest clearing, a tumbledown barn and a viewing point. "This doesn't look like the Font Roja," I said to Eileen, "where's the hotel the restaurant and the spring?" We asked some Spanish people at the viewing point and they redirected us back to the fork where we should have taken the right turn and after a few minutes we arrived at our destination at last. All this time we had been followed by another car whose occupants thought that we knew the way, a case of the blind leading the blind.

The Font Roja was in former times known as a place of pilgrimage and in 1921 a hotel was built to cater for these numerous visitors. Today, this great white building surmounted by a statue of the Virgin Mary has been completely renovated and converted to a study-centre for schools and colleges working in the park. At the side of the study-centre there are car parks, toilets, a restaurant and extensive picnic areas with special barbecue places complete with free wood ready for cooking paella or for frying sausages. The reserve lies some thousand metres above sea level and although the weather was brilliant, we saw snow and ice round here on our February visit. The area is full of unusual plants, shrubs and herbs and houses all kinds of animal life including large birds of prey and even, so we were told, numbers of

The Hill town of Bocairente

wild boars, although perhaps luckily we didn't see any of these. The surroundings here are usually quiet and ideal for walking along the easy footpaths signposted to various summits where there are niveras or great holes, which were used for storing, ice in the days before refrigerators. The food in the park restaurant seemed to reflect the local environment with delicacies such as olleta (stew with rice, vegetables and sausages) and cigons en espinacs (chick peas with spinach).

Still in this area and a few miles to the west of Alcoy is the interesting little town of Bocareinte, which is easily reached, and well worth a visit. As with many of these small Spanish hill towns it is probably better to park just outside and explore the narrow streets on foot, there is convenient parking space here just across the graceful bridge leading to the town centre. By this bridge one sees a noteworthy Monument to the Blanket, a work in iron by the famed Aragonese sculptor Jose Gonzalvo created in homage to the blanket as the town's leading hand-craft and present-day industrial product. One can still purchase a good Bocaireinte blanket in the town, the kind that keeps you warm and lasts forever. Another speciality here is a 'Manta' a kind of poncho or cloak-like blanket with a hole in the middle for the head.

We strolled up the hill from the parking area, passing under an ornate archway with a decidedly Moorish aspect, to the Plaza Mayor with the Municipal Tourist Office on the left-hand side. The Tourist Office is open every morning and a call here is useful to find about the local attractions and about the festival that takes here during the winter. On the day of our February visit the local festival of the Moors and Christians was in progress and a mock plywood castle had been erected in the middle of the Plaza Mayor. It was here in the land of Valencia that the last of the Moors were expelled, some two hundred years after Granada in Andalucia was taken and the festivity at Bocairente is the oldest of its kind and has been declared of special National Tourist interest. At other places the date of the fiesta usually coincides with the feast day of the patron saint of the local town, so the various celebrations are conveniently spaced out throughout the year. The details of the different festivals vary, but they usually last three or four days and involve a religious procession, a spectacular parade and mock battles around an imitation castle made of wood. In Bocairente the feast begins with a night-time procession popularly called 'the night of drums' in which participants with drums and lanterns parade through the streets in honour of their patron saint St Bias. The participants are divided up into nine companies or 'filas' with five Christian companies (Spaniards, Grenadiers, Infantry, Smugglers and Students) and four Moorish (Old Moors, Moroccans, Moorish sailors and Musketeers). There is no distinction between the two protagonists except that more people want to be Moors because their costumes are gaudier with turbans, brightly coloured jackets, animal skins, curved scimitars and even elephant tusks. On the second day of the fiesta there is a spectacular parade around the town to the sound of pasadobles and marches, ending at the Plaza Mayor. The third day is devoted to religious ceremonies and the fourth day features simulated battles between the two warring parties with ear-splitting noise battering the ear drums. Swords are welded, blunderbusses, muskets and cannons are fired indiscriminately using real gunpowder (sometimes with unfortunate results), fireworks and firebombs are thrown and a good time is had by all. At the beginning of the ceremonies the Moors march up to the castle and demand its surrender, this is known as the morning embassy or proclamation. Naturally, the Christians refuse and a furious battle breaks out with the Moors eventually taking the castle.

In the afternoon the roles are reversed, the Christians make the embassy and ultimately succeed in overcoming the Moors. On the last day, following a thanksgiving mass, the Moorish captain is converted to Christianity and there is a final great orgy of fireworks, explosions and gunfire to close the proceedings.

On the coast along the northern Costa Blanca at Moraira the fiesta of the Moors and Christians takes place in June and involves an invasion from the sea and battles around the old castle on the seashore. The main parade here lasts for about three hours and includes companies from all over the region, each company accompanied by its own band with a huge drum carried along on a cart. The costumes are spectacular and there was even a small elephant in the parade one year.

After visiting the Tourist Office in Bocairente and obtaining maps and information Eileen and I decided to walk in the direction of a local historical curiosity, the caves of the Moors. We turned left out of the main square and followed a narrow signposted alleyway past some old woollen mills, these old mills now serve as the headquarters for the companies of the Moors and Christian, really social clubs. The alleyway became a track running towards a gorge with the town sewage works bubbling away merrily on the hillside to the right. On the other side of the valley the caves of the Moors could be seen carved out of the rock-face opposite the medieval town centre. To approach the caves you had to traverse the rough, damp valley floor and cross a stream to the entrance which is some way up the cliff and reached by a rickety iron ladder with widely spaced-out rungs. At the same time as this some Spanish high-school students were making a visit and some of the more adventurous ones had climbed right inside the cave system. We could hear voices coming from different directions and faces kept popping in and out of the cliff openings like an old Rowan and Martin laugh-in T.V. programme.

The Mountain Walkers would have been proud of us as with desperate efforts we managed to pull ourselves up the awkward iron ladder and into the entrance of the caves. The roofs were rather low and we thought that the Moors must have been small or they would have been banging their heads all the time on the rocky ceilings. There didn't appear to be any basic amenities like windows or chimneys and it was all very basic and primitive. We began to feel sorry for the Moors and it was hardly surprising that they all eventually disappeared. After looking round the entrance we extricated ourselves with some difficulty, almost falling out of the caves down the rickety iron ladder and staggered to the other side of the valley where a group of Spanish students had gathered. They were very friendly and seemed amused at our attempts to climb into the cave. We had a conversation with them in English, because it is now the second language in Spain and taught in all the schools. After our exertions in the caves there was still time to visit the old quarter of the town and the bullring cut into the rocks.

Returning towards Alcoy, the road passes the village of Agres which is at the other end of the trail coming from the Singing Gorge. Agres is another village built on a hillside and is the resting place of the holy statue of the Mare de Dieu d'Agres which attracts many pilgrims each year. There is an interesting walk starting from the side of the sanctuary of the holy statue to Mont Cabrer, the third highest peak in the region. The first part of the walk is the hardest, but not too strenuous if taken easily (we managed it all right, although it brought back memories of Paul Robeson singing as he climbed with a caravan

The Sanctuary, Agres

A mountain village

to the high plateau in the old film of 'King Solomon's Mines'). The path is always obvious and there is a hut at the top belonging to Alcoy Mountaineering Club with some well-preserved niveras or ice holes nearby. The return to Agres is merely a downhill saunter along quiet roads.

Club Tabaira

THE SKELETON AND THE SHE DEVIL

At the town of Orihuela on Spain's Costa Blanca, not far from Torrevieja, are two local curiosities. These consist of an almost life sized skeleton and a carving known as the 'Paso de la Diablesa' or she devil because of the ghastly horned woman's face that the artist Nicholas de Busi gave to his creation. No church will give the grisly couple houseroom, so during the year they are given unsanctified sanctuary in the darkest depths of the vaults in the local library. Every Easter the gruesome couple are hauled out of their lair in the library vaults and traipsed around the streets of the town as a warning to the wicked to repent. The horrid couple look almost lifelike and some people have sworn that they have seen them move. If the grisly pair did somehow miraculously come to life, perhaps a situation like this could take place.

One morning shortly before Easter the dustsheets in the dim musty depths of the library cellars began to stir.

"Wake up, wake up Skeleton. It's nearly time for our annual outing again and I hope you remember to behave yourself this year, there was a near-riot when you clacked your teeth at the crowd in the Plaza Mayor last Easter.".

"I promise not to clack my teeth She-devil if you promise not to start waving to the crowd as if you're someone important, who do you think you are, the Queen of Spain?"

"It's just that I don't like to disappoint my public, Skeleton. People expect something a little more sophisticated these days."

"Oh, so it's 'my public' is it now She-devil, and I thought we were a partnership. May I remind you that we're supposed to frighten people

Torrevieja, Costa Blanca

to repent, not to entertain them."

"You worry too much Skeleton, I don't think the authorities care what we do so long as it brings in the tourists. There's a record crowd expected this year and it's all good for business. However, it would be nice to see the town and the river properly. You can't see much from the back of a cart with all the crowds gaping at you. Of course, we can't go out as we are, it would cause panic in the streets."

"You can say that again She-devil. I've been lying here all this year thinking about the same thing myself. If we could get hold of some money, we could buy some second hand coats with a hood and use them for disguises. In the dark you could easily pass for a little old lady and I could resemble a thin bony old man. Then we could walk around Orihuela one evening in complete anonymity."

"But how could we manage all this?"

"As you know it's nearly Holy Week with its processions and penitents. There are lots of dustsheets, old papers and (clothes) down here and someone has even left an old pair of plimpsolls. If I draped myself in plenty of dustsheets, made a pointed hat from the old newspapers with two slits for the eyeholes and put on the plimpsolls I could pass myself off as a penitent. We know the layout of the library here, so you could let me out in the early hours of the morning and I'd have to find somewhere to hide. Later on in the morning I'd come back into town and pose as a penitent outside the Church of Santiago near the Plaza Mayor. People will take me for a living statue like the ones you see in Benidorm or in Torrevieja and put some money in a cap at my feet. When I've got enough money I'll buy some coats with a hood from a nearby market stall. At siesta time I'll just fade away and hide until it gets dark, when I'll return here after the library closes. Then we can disguise ourselves and go for a walk around the town."

"It sounds possible, Skeleton, lets try it out tomorrow."

"Who's that funny looking man wearing sheets and a pointed hat standing outside the church, mummy."

"He's called a penitent, dear."

"What's a penitent, mummy?"

"A penitent is someone who is sorry for doing wrong."

"What has he done wrong?"

"I really don't know, dear."

"Why isn't he moving then?"

"That's because he is posing as a living statue like the ones we saw along the seafront at Benidorm, If you put a coin in his cap he will bow or raise his arm."

"I would like to see him move, let's give him a euro mummy."

"Very well dear, then we must get on."

"Come along dear, why are you waiting."

"I'm just looking back at the living statue, there seemed something very strange about him to me when he raised his arm. Oh look mummy, there's a little doggy coming down the street and it's started sniffing at the statue's legs. Oh, naughty, naughty doggy, it's lifted its leg on the statue's foot and scampered off. Now a bigger dogs coming and it's started sniffing around too. Oh no! The big doggy has grabbed the statue's leg in his jaws and has started to worry it. The doggy must think it's a bone. Oh dear, now the statue has kicked the big dog in the ribs with his other foot and the poor doggy has run off howling down the road. A policeman is coming up now and he's getting out his notebook. Will he arrest the statue mummy? Look, look, the statue has come to life. It's scooped up all the money in the cap and is running away down the street chased by the policeman. It looks funny mummy and people are laughing. Mummy, it's not a statue at all, it really is a skeleton, and I could see its bony legs when it lifted up its sheets to run. Now the policeman has given up the chase and the skeleton is almost out of sight. I've never seen a skeleton running before."

"Nonsense, dear, it's not a skeleton at all, it's just a man in a dark costume painted to look like a skeleton."

"It looked like a real skeleton to me."

"Let me in, let me in She-devil. Oh what a day I've had!"

"At least you seem to have had some success Skeleton, disguised as a peasant carrying a bundle of clothes, you look quite realistic in the darkness."

"Yes, and I've managed to get you a coat and a pair of shoes as well. But to go back to the beginning, I slipped out of the library side door in the early hours without being seen and hid in the town until it was time to take up my pose in the Plaza outside the church of Santiago. Everything went very well at first and I soon had a some coins in my cap. Then, just before siesta time a little dog arrived and began sniffing around my legs, then the wretched pest lifted its leg up on my foot before running off. As if this wasn't bad enough, shortly afterwards a much larger dog appeared and began sniffing around as well and I thought it was going to do the same thing as the first dog. Instead of that however, thinking it was a bone, the dog grabbed my leg in its jaws and started worrying it. Fearful that the dog would run off with my leg and leave me stranded, I managed to land a good kick on the creature's ribs with my other foot. The dog yelped, let go of my leg and ran off down the street with its tail between its legs. All this attracted the attention of a policeman standing at the corner of the Plaza and he came up, notebook in hand to make enquiries. This was when my nerve failed and I panicked. Scooping up the capful of money and lifting my skirts I fled down the street, hotly pursued by the policeman. Luckily the penitents pointed hat stayed on or my cover would have been blown. Of course, because I'm not human I didn't get tired so I soon outran the policeman. I kept on running for quite some time until I reached the countryside where I had a piece of luck. First I found a pair of shoes on a rubbish dump then outside a village I came across some clothes including a coat that had been left on some bushes to dry. I selected what I wanted and left money for the villagers with a message scratched on the ground nearby; 'Please buy some new clothes for Easter'. Then I threw away the dust sheets and the pointed hat, disguised myself as a peasant and crept back here when it got dark and the library closed and you let me in."

"My goodness, Skeleton, you've had a lot of adventures. Just give me a minute to put on the coat and shoes and we'll venture out into town."

"It's lovely and peaceful down here by the riverbank, Skeleton, but do you think it's safe so late at night?"

"I admit it is lonely, but no one in his right mind would dare to try anything with us."

"I hope you're right, Skeleton, because I can see a suspicious looking character lurking in the shadows and he's coming this way."

"Buenos noches, senor and senora, you are out very late at night for two old people. I am desperate and I have a knife, stand still, hand over all your money or it will be the worst for you."

"Get lost, hombre, you don't know who you're dealing with, show him you horns, She-devil."

"Argh. Madre de Mia!"

"Well done She-devil, he's passed out, but we'll soon bring him round. The Rio Segura is running very low just now so if we throw him in he won't drown. Grab him by the ankles and heave him in. On the count of three, over he goes." 'Splash, Argh'.

"Now we can get on with our walk in peace and I'll be content for the next hundred years, but we'll have to get rid of these clothes in a skip before we go back inside the library."

From the COSTA BLANCA NEWS.

Strange happenings in Orihuela

The authorities here have discounted reports that a member of the Civil Guard tried to arrest a skeleton in the Plaza outside the church of Santiago and unsuccessfully chased it into the countryside. The reported incident has been put down to overwrought imagination and the effects of the local strong wine. The Civil Guard in question has been suspended from duty, pending medical reports. The evidence of a witness to the event, an eight-year-old child, has been discounted as 'unreliable' whilst a large dog also involved in the incident is being treated at the local vets. In an seemingly unrelated incident, a local petty criminal in a state of severe shock and distress, was pulled out of the Rio Segura very late last night. At first he was unable to give a coherent account about what happened, but in time he recovered enough to babble something about being thrown into the river by a skeleton and a she-devil. This explanation is being put down to hallucinations caused by an overdose of drugs.

However, a report from an outlying village of an apparently miraculously substitution of some old clothes by a substantial sum of genuine money has been confirmed as true by reliable sources. The money was accompanied by a message telling the villagers to buy some new clothes for Easter.

Strangely enough, when the vaults of Orihuela library were inspected some time later nothing really suspicious was discovered. The Skeleton and the She-devil were still there, but the dustsheets looked as if they had been disturbed. Also, there were the remains of a battered pair of plimsolls lying on the floor and the Skeleton seemed to have a hideous grin on its face.

These reports have created great interest in the annual Easter procession due to take place shortly and record crowds are expected this year. There much speculation as to whether the Skeleton will apparently clack its teeth at the crowd again or the She-devil will wave herr arm as allegedly occurred last year.

In conclusion, it is reported that a very well known international firm has bought the marketing rights for the Skeleton and the She-devil from Orihuela council for a large sum of money. Skeleton T-shirts and She-devil perfume will soon be in the shops.

Dique de Levante Walk

LEARNING SPANISH

It is said that a good way to understand the culture of a country is to learn its language, so with this object in mind I began to learn Spanish. Unfortunately, learning a language is more easily said than done and for me it began an Odyssey lasting several years of evening classes and study. During this time it was sometimes hard to leave the house on a dark winter evening, but in compensation the classes were enjoyable and in the end the effort was worthwhile.

At first I tried phrase books that contained 'useful' sentences to be learnt parrot fashion to suit different situations and circumstances. These sentences didn't seem all that relevant or likely to be of much use in everyday life, even if you could memorise the words. Most of the sentences contained obscure grammar and were written in sequence like the synopsis of a story that usually built up to a disastrous climax. For example, in the section entitled 'Swimming' the first sentence to memorise started with the innocuous question 'Shall we swim?' This was followed by the alarming 'Swim and help him, he has gone under!' and finally 'Hang on to the lifeline!' Under the heading, 'Sports' there were phrases like, 'The boat is heeling over and is sinking' and 'The yacht has capsized' whilst 'Mountaineering' contained the cheerful, 'they lost their way and a rescue party has gone out to find them' concluding with 'the injured mountaineers were brought down on stretchers.' The heading 'Golf' contained so called useful phrases that it would be almost impossible to learn by heart like, 'the women amateur champion sank her ball like a professional' and the comical sounding, 'try not to falter on the fairways' (trate de no fallar en los recorridos).

The material in this book reminded me of the classic sentence, 'my postillion has been struck by lightening' presuming you know what a postillion is. One wonders if even in the olden days a postillion ever was struck by lightening and if the sentence was ever used. If it was, I feel sorry for the unfortunate postillion and hope he survived the accident. Although this Spanish phrase book was published fairly recently, it contained information now completely obsolete. In the section devoted to hotels it had the following sentence, 'I am going to clap my hands to see if the night-watchman comes along,' which must be a useful thing to know in present day Benidorm. Also, the sequence of the printed sentences could be rather unfortunate as well. In the section devoted to 'Correspondence' the sentence, 'I was very pleased to hear the news of your engagement' (marriage) was immediately followed be, 'my sincere condolences' and 'may I express my deepest sympathy.'

The teaching standards of the language classes varied, some of the beginners classes were oversubscribed and resembled social get-togethers, although the numbers fell off as the year proceeded. Later classes run by the Colleges or Universities would be taught in Spanish with assessments, exams and a certificate at the end. You could get quite familiar with some class members during the year, only to lose contact at the end of the course. A case of ships that pass in the night. Language tapes could be useful, but you need a lot of self-discipline to stick to the work because there always seems to be so many other things to do.

After some time I had progressed far enough to be able to read Spanish newspapers. I used to buy the popular 'El Pais' and was amused by a full-page weekly cartoon feature called 'The Adventures of Cutlass'. Cutlass was a cowboy with an ironic sense of humour, but had various enemies including some Wild West desperadoes and the tribe of the Sioux Red Indians. The story would begin with Cutlass calling his faithful horse Silver to action.

"Whoa! Silver, let's go out and look for some adventures." However, by three o'clock in the afternoon nothing had happened, then suddenly a voice rings out.

"Give up Cutlass, I have allied myself with the Sioux to destroy you, surrender now!"

"Vile traitor, never," replies Cutlass and draws his revolver. Then follows a battle with a hail of bullets and clouds of arrows. Finally, at the end of the battle Cutlass exclaims, "Oh dear, I have killed the entire tribe of the Sioux, mind you, it was in self-defence." Later on a young woman appears.

"Oh Cutlass, they told me you were dead!"

"No."

"Oh Cutlass, perhaps one day we will meet again?"

"Perhaps."

As Cutlass makes his way home he encounters a friend who asks:- "What kind of a day did you have Cutlass?"

"Well, it was a bit boring in the morning, but better in the afternoon." Stories like this used to appear every week in the 'El Pais' Spanish newspaper.

One book that I did find useful, but which must be out of print now, is 'Spanish for Fun' published in 1966 by Leslie Charteris the author of the 'Saint' novels. But whatever your method of learning, even a basic vocabulary is useful and gives you confidence in a foreign country.

ERNESTO – A DIVERSION

In the course of some background reading about Spain, I came across an old book called 'The Glories of Spain' by Charles W. Wood published in 1901. The book describes the author's travels around northern Spain just before the turn of the century in 1898, including a visit to the town of Gerona. It was here that he made the acquaintance of a Spanish lady and here son Ernesto who lived in a house opposite their hostel. Although the style of writing seems rather old-fashioned today, I would like to include these extracts from the book as a tribute to an early travel writer.

Immediately opposite our casement was a small draper's shop presided over by an industrious feminine genius. She was up betimes and worked as if she had taken to heart all the proverbs of Solomon. A short, dark women of the true Spanish type, bright, active, and not above all manners of work, for she swept her pavement diligently and arranged her wares; doing all with a certain natural grace that was not without its charm.

We thought her a young widow struggling for existence, but when all the work was done and comfortably arranged, a husband appeared upon the scene; evidently a lord of creation who looked upon women and especially wives as born to labour. It was their portion under the sun. She had no doubt grown used to this state of affairs and accepted it as one of life's penances.

"I hope you have slept well," we heard her say with the slightest tinge of sarcasm – the street was so narrow as to bring them almost within half a dozen yards of us. "I have been up these two hours whilst

Ernesto's mother

you were serenely unconscious," veiling her head in a graceful mantilla. "Yet you hardly seemed refreshed," as he yawned lazily.

"Cara mia, you are an admirable women and the best of wives. I admit that without your aid life would go hardly with me. But to you work is a pleasure and I would not deprive you of it for the world."

By this time the mantilla was adjusted and the little dark women swept good temperedly out of the shop. She looked up, saw us gazing in her direction and her smile disclosed the whitest of teeth. "Ah senor, you have heard our conjugal good morning. It is always the same. Fate has been hard with us women. The weaker vessel we get terribly imposed on by our masters. Now I go to church to pray for a blessing upon my work and reformation to my lord. Not that he is bad or unkind or tyrannical as husbands go – only incorrigibly lazy. Oh, you that is true, Stephano."

Upon which the little lady – she was quite lady-like in spite of the swept pavement and the hard work – made us a court curtsey, flourished a farewell to her caro esposo and passed swiftly and gracefully down the street. It is said that only Spanish women know how to walk, and there is some truth in the proverb.

Later on as the author and his party explored the town, they bumped into the little lady again.

It was now that we saw our industrious and amiable senora preparing for the fair. Again the mantilla was being gracefully arranged. The little lady, very properly, had evidently no idea of neglecting the good looks that nature had bestowed upon her.

"Ah, senor," as we stopped with a polite greeting, "for a whole week this fair is the upsetting and devastation of the town. It comes with all its shows and shoutings; distracts our attention; we might as well close the shutters for all the business that is done; finally it walks off with all our spare money. And who is a bit better for it?"

But madam's grievance was evidently not very deep-seated for she laughed as she adjusted the folds of her mantilla more becomingly, and looking across at a mirror could only confess herself satisfied with her bewitching appearance.

Near her stood a good-looking boy of some fourteen years who evidently just then thought the attractions of the fair far more important than his mother's adorning. He was impatient to be off.

"Calm yourself my treasure," she remonstrated. "The day is yet young. The chestnuts will not all be roasted, nor brazen trumpets all sold. These are inexhaustible like the snows of the Sierra. Oh! Youth, youth, with all its capacities!" she dramatically added. "Ah, senor, you will think me very old, when you see me the mother of this great boy!"

We gallantly protested that she was under a delusion; he must be her brother.

"My son, senor, my son. I married at sixteen, when I was almost such a child as he, and I really do feel more like his sister than his mother. Alas! If I had only waited a few years longer I might have chosen more wisely; perhaps found a husband to keep me instead of my keeping him. Marriage is a lottery."

We suggested that every cloud has its silver lining. "True senor, and after all if I did not draw the highest number, neither did I fall upon the lowest. This dear youth too is a consolation. He is fond of swords and trumpets, but shall never be a soldier. I have long had the money put by for a substitute in case he should be unlucky in the draft. For that matter, Heaven has prospered my industry and in a humble way we are at ease."

This recalled the scene witnessed earlier in the morning and the appointment half made with the colonel for the morrow (the Spanish/American war was in progress at this time).

"Evidently you do not approve of conscription, madame, which today seems to be running hand in hand with the revels of the fair."

"I see conscription as a necessary evil," returned madame, "for without it you would not get soldiers; but you will never persuade me any good can come of it. So, Ernesto, never fix your attentions on a military life, for it can never be, never shall be. I would sooner make you a priest, though I haven't the least ambition that way either."

To do the boy justice, he seemed quite ready to yield, laughed at the idea of priesthood, and if fond of fond of swords and trumpets, his military ardour went no further. If one might judge, a civil life would be his choice, and possibly a successful one for he seemed to inherit his mother's energy with her dark eyes and brilliant colouring. But for the moment the fair and only the fair was the object of his desires. This was in accordance with the fitness of things. He was at an age which comes once only, with swift wings, when life has no alloy and happiness lies in gratifying the moods and fancies of the moment.

"Now I am ready," said the mother, evidently very happy herself. "Ah, senor, you are too good," as we slipped a substantial sum of money into the boy's hand and bade him buy his mother a fairing (a brooch) and himself chestnuts and ambitions. "But," his mother continued, "after all the pleasure of conferring happiness is the most exquisite in the world. There is nothing like it. So perhaps I should envy, not chide you."

They went off together, the boy taking his mother's arm with the confidential affection and good understanding so often seen abroad. To him the world was still a paradise, and his mother head of all good angels. Les beaux jours de la vie – short-lived and eternally remembered. So, parents, indulge your children but do not spoil them. The one is quite possible without the other.

It was to be a day of encounters. We followed our happy pair down the deserted street, admiring the graceful walk of the mother, the boy's tall, straight, well-nit form and light footstep as they disappeared round the corner leading to the noisy scene of the action.

Some time later the author's party found themselves in the vicinity of Gerona's fair.

We joined the crowd and presently felt a tug at our elbow. It was Ernesto with radiant face, his hands full of chestnuts freely offered and accepted. We found it easy to persuade ourselves that the indigestible horrors were excellent.

"Ernesto, you are taking liberties," said his mother as the boy took our arm to confide his purchases. A Rhinestone brooch for his mother that Mrs Malaprop would have declared quite an object of bigotry and virtue; a wonderful knife for himself, full of sharp blades and secret springs. A purse capable of holding gold, and a pocket book that would soon become dropsical with the boy's treasures. Finally, from the innermost recess of a trousers' pocket, he produced for an instant – a catapult; to be held a profound secret from his mother.

"It keeps her awake at night," he confided; "and when she does get to sleep she dreams of smashed windows and murdered cats. Now I never smash windows, though I do go for the cats when I have a chance. It does them no harm. If I hit them, you hear a thud like the sound from a drum, the cats are not overfed in these parts – but instead of tumbling down dead, they just yowl and scoot off like mad."

"Perhaps they die afterwards, Ernesto, of fractured liver or broken heart."

This was at once negatived.

"Oh no, cats haven't livers and hearts like human beings. Their insides are nothing but India rubber. You can't kill a cat, if one fell the top of San Felieu Cathedral, it would get up, shake its paws and scuttle off."

We noted this revelation, intending to bring it before the University Faculty on our to England, which evidently still gropes in Egyptian darkness. The catapult was restored to safe depths, and before long many a domestic tabby would be missing; there would be widowed cats and orphaned kittens in many a household.

Then Ernesto, drawing us under an arcade, insisted upon fastening his mother's mantilla with the new brooch that we might all admire the flashing stones.

"I believe they have made a mistake and these are real diamonds," he cried excitedly, kissing his mother and duly admiring the effect. "And I haven't spent half my pocket money yet."

"Thanks to you senor," said the happy mother, "I was his first thought. He bought me the brooch before he would look at a knife or a chestnut. It shall be kept amongst my treasures."

She was evidently almost as happy and as light-hearted as the boy, her eyes flashing with proud affection. No great care haunted her life in spite of the conjugal good morning.

"Confess that your lot is favoured," we said, "and you would not change your lazy husband if you had the chance. Confess you adore him and are to be envied."

"Well, senor, you are not my father-confessor," she laughed, "but I will confess to you all the same. I admit I would rather bear the ills I have than fly to those of which I know nothing," unconsciously quoting Shakespeare.

"Then the conjugal good-morning must be a little sweetened. It is dangerous to play with edged tools."

Again she laughed, free from anxiety.

"We understand each other senor. If I received him too amiably he would not appear on the scene till twelve o'clock. Not that I really mind, but it would be a bad example to Ernesto. The boy, however, takes after me. Never will grass grow under his feet."

Ernest was impatient to be off, he must surely act up to the proverb today.

"Now for the shows," cried the lad. "We are losing too much time here. I smell roasted chestnuts, but their flavour is better. We must cross the iron bridge and get to the shows. I want to hear the lions roar and administer cayenne lozenges to the monkeys. It is great fun to see them. You must often have done the same, senor?"

We virtuously disowned the impeachment. But he was full of harmless mischief, after the manner of boys healthy in mind and body; free and open in his thoughts and ways. A few minutes later we found ourselves in the market place listening to the clown who had used superhuman exertions the night before and was still in excellent health and spirits.

"There is Jose, your landlord's son, senor, looking to right and left," said madame, in the interval between two deafening trumpet blasts. "Probably searching for you. Ah! He sees us." The tall, slight young man was making his way through the few remaining stalls in the market. These sold fruit and were altogether neglected. Gerona did not shine in that department.

"I have been looking for you everywhere," said our young host as he came up, bowing politely after the fashion of his country. "I thought, senor, you might want me to pilot you about the town; but you are in the hands of a fairer guide, and I am not needed."

Joseph had evidently not pursued his studies at Tours for nothing and was beginning to turn compliments.

"On the contrary, we shall be glad of your company," we replied. "Ernesto and his mother are going in to hear the lions roar and administer delicacies to the monkeys. And having no ambition to shake in our shoes or to be taken up for cruelty to animals, we would rather explore the antiquities of Gerona under your care. So you appear at the right moment."

"Ah, senor, do come in," pleaded Ernesto, "I should enjoy it so much more. And you would shriek with delight when you saw the antics of the monkeys eating cayenne."

"Ernesto, you are incorrigible," we interrupted, laughing. "We decline the risk; and whilst detesting monkeys, we have a conscience. Yours evidently has still to be awakened. But you may come and tell us your experiences at the hotel later on – that is if you are still at large."

So the boy, taking his mother's arm, boldly mounted the steps and with a final happy nod, and flourishing a small packet of cayenne lozenges, he disappeared beyond the curtain. How the lions would roar or the monkeys receive the indignity remained to be seen. Ernesto was not wanting in purpose and might be trusted to do his best.

Regrettably, after a visit that was only too short, the time came for the party to leave Gerona.

The afternoon shadows were lengthening as we went back through the quiet streets to the hotel. All the brilliant glory of the day had departed. These repeated farewells were depressing, yet not quite over, for as we approached the Fonda who should be standing at their own front door but Ernesto and his mother. We had not met them since the previous day when they had disappeared within the lion's den and we had gone round to the reeds and the river.

"Ernesto! How is this? Why are you not at school?"

"School, senor!" opening very wide eyes. "Fair week is a holiday. We should have a revolution if they attempted school upon us. For this one week in the year we change places with our fathers and mothers, pastors and teachers. They obey and we command."

"We congratulate you on this topsy-turvy state of affairs, but as you are strong, be merciful. Remember that Black Monday comes, Cinderella went back to her rags at midnight; you must go back to school and good work. And the monkeys? You are still at large, we feared the opposite, as you had not brought us your report."

"Oh! I brought it senor; but it was rather late, and Senor Lasoli said you were at the opera. You should have seen the monkeys!" And here he went into convulsions at the recollection of the performance. "They couldn't understand what was inside the lozenges to bite their tongues so! First they would take a nibble; then rub the lozenge on their arms; then a whole torrent of monkey swearing and lozenge rubbing because it kept on burning and biting. I thought I should die with laughing."

From the way he was laughing now, it seemed doubtful whether all danger was over.

"But that is not the worst, senor," said the mother, at length making herself heard. "Will you believe that the boy has a wretched catapult in his pocket, and there will be any number of broken windows and assassinated cats in the town. I don't know what will become of us. If there is one thing I dread more than another, it is a catapult. They are the implements of the devil."

"There is absolutely no fear," laughed Ernesto. "I never broke a window in my life – at least, hardly ever. As for cats, they are quite outside the law of murder. A dead cat is as rare as a dead donkey. Are you really going today, senor? Then I shall have no more pleasure at the fair, though this year it has been better than usual. The lions roared like thunder and the monkeys accepted all the lozenges. They were punished for their greediness. But will you come back to spend a whole month in Gerona? And if you allowed me, I would take you to some of the excursions in the neighbourhood. There are any number within twenty miles; ruined churches and deserted monasteries. I don't care much about them myself, but I know many who do. It seems to me that a good show and a handful of chestnuts are worth all the wretched old ruins in the world."

In spite of this vandalism, we assured Ernesto that when we spent a month in Gerona he should have the honour of escorting us, provided it was not in school time. He wished to bind us to a given date, thereby showing a talent for business, but we refused to be committed to the inevitable. We left mother and son together, a picture of domestic happiness. As we disappeared under the archway of the hotel, Ernesto held up his catapult in triumph, successfully parrying his mother's attempt to obtain possession of the forbidden weapon. She evidently looked upon it as only one degree below an infernal machine.

It would be really interesting to know what happened to Ernesto and what kind of a life he led in the future. Hopefully fate would be kind to him and it would be nice to think that his ancestors still live in Gerona and enjoy visiting whatever has succeeded the great Fair.

Molino del Aqua Park

SOME FRIENDS

The location of the casa pequena up a steep hill about a mile outside the village at Tabaira made the use of a car almost essential, especially in the heat of July and August. This is how we made the acquaintance of Antonio, the proprietor of the local car-hire firm 'Mr Car'. When we first met Antonio he had just started up in business and lived with his wife and family above a bar in the village. Spanish bars stay open late and are quite noisy so life must have been difficult for Antonio and his family just then. Antonio could speak good English and was always cheerful, even if he had spent the previous night driving between Valencia and Alicante. We didn't always have our own transport, but if Antonio saw us plodding up the hill in the heat of the day, he always stopped to ask if we wanted a lift. The logo of the firm 'Mr Car' depicted a man in a dinner jacket wearing a bow tie, a monocle and a top hat resembling a kind of Bertie Wooster character from the books of P. G. Wodehouse who would have been out of date a hundred years before. Maybe 'Mr Car' represented some kind of crazy Spanish notion of a typical English lord or an aristocrat. In the advertising material 'Mr Car' wore his top hat and monocle all the time, when arriving at the airport and even when relaxing on the beach, when the top hat was deposited on the back of a deckchair. Whatever the psychology behind the advert it seemed to work because Antonio's firm prospered. In time he opened a spacious office on the main road near the sea front and employed more staff including his wife. We used Antonio's firm for many years, until we moved away from Moraira and eventually lost contact.

Quite often we didn't know the real names of people we used to see

WE COVER ALL THE COSTA BLANCA

MR CAR S.L.
RENT A CAR

around the neighbourhood or in the shops, but identified them by some characteristic feature or even by the name of their dog. Frank was a chance acquaintance we met in the village and was always accompanied by an Alsatian dog, so he became known to us as Frank with the Alsatian. We never knew much about Frank except that he came from south London and had been a taxi driver. We often saw him over the years and used to look out for him in the village, he was very pleasant and brought us up to date with all the local news as well supplying useful information. This situation went on for some years until we arrived on one occasion to find he wasn't around anymore. We asked about him at the 'Cap d'Or' bar where we all used to meet and heard the sad news that Frank had died in London during the previous winter.

Harry was a resident who lived down the hill a little way from us and was one of the first owners on the urbanisation. As a resident, he used to look after things for absentee owners, holding keys, paying bills and caring for villas. We used to see him walking up the road brandishing sheaves of papers and complaining bitterly about the local utility companies.

"Just look at this," he complained, "there are electric bills here going back months and the office have no idea what they're doing. If an account gets overlooked you have to go to a certain bank, get a receipt and trail back to the office. At one stage Harry and his wife became live-in caretakers at a luxury villa owned by a rich American lady half way down the hill to the village. Sadly, the arrangement didn't work out as the American lady became too demanding. In the end I believe Harry's wife died overseas and he returned to Britain to live in Essex.

Over the years we got different people to help us with our on going battle with the garden and this was how we met Paddy, who was Irish as his name implies. In spite of a foot impediment, Paddy was an active member of the Mountain Walkers group and had absolutely no fear of heights. One day we asked for his help in cutting down some tall pine saplings in the garden, which were getting far too big and threatening to get completely out of control.

"I'll sort them out for you, leave them to me" promised Paddy. He arrived at our garden later in the day and after surveying the trees, proceeded to climb like Tarzan to the top of the biggest of the pine saplings.

"Be careful, don't fall," we implored him anxiously from down below on the drive, not being insured for a fatality.

"Sure it's a fine view from up here, you can see for miles," replied Paddy unperturbed, swaying precariously about in the wind from his perch at the top of the pine tree.

"I'll get rid of this big branch first," he called out and lopped it clean off with one wild swing of his axe. The heavy branch tumbled down onto the garden wall, breaking the decorative breezeblock topping, but we were thankful that Paddy hadn't crashed down with the bough as well. "That's wonderful," we shouted up through the branches, "it's improved things tremendously, there's no need to do any more." "Are you sure?" replied Paddy, disappointedly, "I'm really enjoying it up here."

"Quiet sure," we said firmly and breathed a sigh of relief as he descended safely.

Hermy lived in a villa on our side of the road just down the hill. She was a retired nurse of Austrian origin and an animal lover who adopted the role of an unofficial R.S.P.C.A. in the district. She looked after stray cats and dogs and owned a shorthaired dog, which she named Coffee.

Unfortunately, like similar people, Hermy was not an expert at training animals and imagined that they could all understand English. She continued to over indulge her charges with misplaced kindness and didn't seem to have much control over Coffee, which used to do as it pleased. The kitchen sink in her villa was filled with pots and pans, which she used to prepare the animal's food. It was a worry if she invited you for a meal that you could get the dog's dinner by mistake and that the stew you were enjoying could have been meant for Coffee.

Owning a pet in Spain can be a problem if you have to return home at short notice. Catherine lived in the villa on the opposite side of the road to Hermy and owned a valuable pedigree cat called Thomas. When Catherine had to return to Britain in an emergency she made arrangements for someone to come up from the village every day to feed Thomas. The cat was supposed to stay inside the villa but of course, soon after Catherine's departure, it sneaked out of the back door and ran off into the woods. Frantic searches were organised by the neighbours to try and find Thomas, but no amount of pussy-'pussying' 'could bring him to light. The day of Catherine's return drew nearer and people became resigned to the fact that Thomas was lost for good. Then, as you can guess, miraculously, just before his owner returned the cat reappeared as if by magic. How the cat knew its owner was coming back the next day was a mystery, perhaps cats have a sixth sense that we don't know about. Catherine knew nothing about all this and was overjoyed when she was reunited with Thomas.

"Thank you so much for looking after him," she thanked the relieved carer, "I've never seen him looking so healthy."

As well as the British, we got to know quite a few of the local Spanish people, apart from the two Antonio's, at the banks shops and restaurants. These people always remembered us from visit to visit and greeted us like old friends.

MOVING ON

Moraira is a lovely place and we really enjoyed our time there but nothing lasts forever. As the years passed by and we grew older the steep hill from the village became more tiring to climb and the garden with all its pine trees harder to manage. We spent money to have some of the pine trees cut down, but the remaining trees just kept growing bigger. In addition, some of the people we used to know had moved on or had died so we decided that this would be a good time to look for something easier and more convenient.

A few days later we contacted Antonio who had prospered over the years and was now a partner in an important construction firm with its head offices in Moraira. We had kept in touch with him over the years and his firm had done some work for us on the 'casa pequena' fairly recently. Antonio welcomed us as old friends and showed us into his impressive office. The walls of the office displayed photographs of a bygone Moraira showing simple fishermen's cottages, a primitive bar and a rough track leading down to a tiny harbour. These photographs looked ancient as if they dated from the early 20th century, yet surprisingly most of them were of fairly recent origin; times around here had changed so fast.

After exchanging mutual greetings we began to explain the purpose of our meeting.

"As you know, Antonio, we've been here a long time. Unfortunately our location up the steep hill in Tabaira is beginning to get too inconvenient and we would like something nearer to the village."

"We might have something to interest you," Antonio replied, "we are building an estate of modern houses at a development called 'Los

Moraira

Pelicanos' which is quite near the sea-front at the Cap de Moraira. We don't build the old style of villa anymore with their high ceilings, exposed wooden beams and wrought iron work. The older type of house looked very picturesque but they weren't really functional, being difficult to heat in winter and needing more decorating. The latest houses have much better insulation and are easier to maintain. However, I must warn you that prices are higher nearer to the coast and that Moraira has grown more popular and expensive since you first came."

As a long time friend we knew that Antonio would give us a fair deal so we agreed to go and have a look at the 'Los Pelicanos' development very soon. The next day Antonio met us outside the offices of the building company in a large, up to date German car as he had done many years before in Benidorm and drove us to the estate situated a short distance behind the beach at Portet beneath the Cap de Moraira. The urbanisation consisted of a tiered semi-circle of villas and houses grouped around a terraced amphitheatre, facing a large swimming pool with long distance views down the valley to the sea front. There was a large space of building land left by the road for any future commercial developments and all the facilities seemed fairly close at hand. The house we inspected was light, roomy and well designed with just a small garden and no encroaching pine forest.

"As you see," explained Antonio, "it's only about a five minute walk to the beach. At the moment the nearest supermarket at Portet is only open in the summer, but there are bars and restaurants facing the beach and the village is not too far away."

The estate of houses looked impressive and we were sorely tempted. Although a house at 'Los Pehcanos' would have been suitable for our needs, as Antonio had said, the properties were not cheap and prices were higher nearer to the coast. However, we were certainly very interested and got as far as viewing building materials and offering to pay a deposit but somehow the deal fell through. This was around the time when the property market in Spain was still stagnant before the great boom of the early years of the century and we were concerned about the financial situation and how safe our money would be. So as in the holiday T.V. property programmes, we decided that we liked the area but have to think things over.

Later on Antonio showed us another development of linked town houses called 'Los Olivios' further inland along the Benitachell road.

"These houses are excellent value, easily maintained and within your price range. They are selling well and will not be available for very long," he informed us.

"Yes, they are very attractive," we agreed, "but they are a long way inland and a car would be essential. If we came out here there would be no improvement on our situation at Tabaira."

Although of no interest to us, Antonio was perfectly correct and the units soon sold out. We continued to look around various localities nearby, but didn't see anything we really liked.

The 'casa pequena' was put up for sale with a firm connected to Antonio's son Peta and was eventually sold to some German people. It was sad to say goodbye to everyone at Tabaira after so many years and even our old friend the ancient carob-bean tree seemed to droop as we left for the last time. Of course, Hans came out to wave us good-bye and remarked that, "things won't be the same around here when you've gone and I won't have anyone working in the garden to watch and advise." Hermy of the animal sanctuary said she was sorry we leaving because we had been one of the first wave of visitors at the urbanisation and soon there wouldn't be any of the original owners left. In a way we were sorry to be leaving the house and garden as well, but circumstances had changed so much. Funnily enough, when we paid a return visit to Tabaira some years later, the garden of our old house was exactly as we had left it with the carob tree thriving and the stump of 'Old Sequoia' still visible.

FRESH FIELDS

After about another eighteen months events began to change once more. The Spanish property market revived and adverts began to appear in magazines and newspapers again. By this time we had begun to miss Spain, so when an advert appeared for a property exhibition in our local newspaper we decided to go and take a look. The urbanisation in question was situated at the town of Torrevieja to the south of Alicante and the properties looked interesting, so yet again we booked a package holiday to Benidorm as our base for viewing, which seemed the cheapest option.

So it came about that one rainy November day we found ourselves driving down the autopista to visit the resorts south of Alicante airport, Santa Pola, Guardamar and Torrevieja. This was our first visit to the southern region or Vega Baja of the Costa Blanca and the terrain here was much flatter than around Moraira with long sandy beaches backed by pinewoods and the shape of Tabarca Island just visible on the horizon. We made contact with the local estate agents, but didn't see anything we really liked. In compensation we met two people from home who were also interested in the area and who remained good friends for the next ten years. However, on the return journey just outside Torrevieja along the main road we saw a development that was just being constructed. The first phase of the development had been completed and almost sold out, but the second phase was in the planning stage and properties were up for sale. Although technically inside the boundary of Guardamar, the development was just outside the town of La Mata. The construction consisted of two storey apartments, without a garden, behind the sand dunes and near the beach.

There was a pleasant view of the pine forest but the trees were at a safe distance away and someone else's responsibility, unlike the situation at Moraira. The town of La Mata was only a short distance away and there was a frequent bus service to Torrevieja itself with the Costa Azul bus line. This development seemed to tick all the boxes, so disregarding all our good advice about buying property in Spain we signed up for an apartment off-plan and paid a large deposit. This was the second time that we had taken a dangerous gamble in Spain. At first everything seemed to go well, but then a few months later had we an awful shock. A telephone call came from our Spanish agent. "I'm terribly sorry to tell you this, but the building work on your property has stopped and the work is only half completed." For the space of two weeks we thought we had lost all our money. But then we found out the true situation. The properties had been marketed at a very low price and the building firm wanted more money. This same firm changed its name and offered to complete the work for more money. We duly paid the extra cost, work started again and in the end we got our apartment facing the pinewoods as planned.

Meanwhile our neighbourhood friends who we met on the visit had bought a house at Punta Prima south of Torrevieja and had become permanent residents. We used to see them on our visits at a popular bar/restaurant called the 'Nautilus' along the coast. Inland just behind the apartment are situated the two extensive lakes of Torrevieja, which are used for the production of salt, but also have vineyards and citrus groves around their banks. The first lake also served as a bird sanctuary and there is a visitor centre. There are pleasant walks around the lakes which both have a circumference of about eighteen miles. The first lake accepts water from the sea where it is condensed. This water is then pumped into the second lake where it is processed into salt at the bottom end. This condensed water is also said to have therapeutic qualities and there is talk of creating a health spa. One day we walked near the lake and waded into the water. Nearby we met a man who claimed that the water could cure arthritis. "You see my dog running around, well he had difficulty walking until I put him in the water and now he's completely better." Some people come with bottles to take the water home.

We stayed in La Mata for the next ten years until circumstances changed again. We were getting older and also became concerned about the amount of building work going on up and down the coast. We couldn't see how this amount of development could be sustained. In the end we sold out to some Dutch people, but continued to visit the area to see our English and Spanish friends, usually staying at the La Zenia hotel on Flamenca beach.

Hotel la Zenia, Torrevuija
This is where we go now when we visit our friends in Spain

ACKNOWLEDGEMENTS

We made many friends in Spain, although, sadly some are no longer with us.

In Moraira our very good friends, Harold and Rita, were residents who helped us a great deal.

Also our neighbour, Hermy, who looked after the dog, Coffee.

Antonio Tro Fluxa and his son, Peta, of Construction Moraira, and Antonio of 'Mr Car'.

In Le Mata, Tracey on the Roscasa development. Hurst and Brigitta, Else and Ignace Stevenz from Holland, Jan and Gerrie next door to us, and especially José Jimanez Tirado, the manager of La Mata supermarket.

Finally, Brian and Ann, plus Margaret of La Zenia.

Juan Aparicio Promenade